Santander & Picos de Europa

Andy Symington

Credits

Footprint credits

Editor: Felicity Laughton
Production and layout: Emma Bryers
Maps: Kevin Feeney

Managing Director: Andy Riddle
Content Director: Patrick Dawson
Publisher: Alan Murphy
Publishing Managers: Felicity Laughton,
Jo Williams, Nicola Gibbs
Marketing and Partnerships Director:
Liz Harper
Marketing Executive: Liz Eyles
Trade Product Manager: Diane McEntee
Account Managers: Paul Bew, Tania Ross
Advertising: Renu Sibal, Elizabeth Taylor
Finance: Phil Walsh

Photography credits

Front cover: Tomas Pavelka/ Dreamstime
Back cover: Juan Pablo Fuentes Serrano/
Dreamstime

Printed in Great Britain by CPI Antony Rowe,
Chippenham, Wiltshire

MIX
Paper from
responsible sources
FSC® C013604
www.fsc.org

Every effort has been made to ensure that
the facts in this guidebook are accurate.
However, travellers should still obtain advice
from consulates, airlines, etc, about travel
and visa requirements before travelling.
The authors and publishers cannot accept
responsibility for any loss, injury or
inconvenience however caused.

Publishing information

Footprint *Focus Santander & Picos de Europa*
1st edition
© Footprint Handbooks Ltd
April 2012

ISBN: 978 1 908206 61 9
CIP DATA: A catalogue record for this book
is available from the British Library

® Footprint Handbooks and the Footprint
mark are a registered trademark of
Footprint Handbooks Ltd

Published by Footprint
6 Riverside Court
Lower Bristol Road
Bath BA2 3DZ, UK
T +44 (0)1225 469141
F +44 (0)1225 469461
footprinttravelguides.com

Distributed in the USA by Globe Pequot
Press, Guilford, Connecticut

The content of Footprint *Focus Santander
& Picos de Europa* has been taken directly
from Footprint's *Northern Spain Handbook*
which was researched and written by
Andy Symington.

Contents

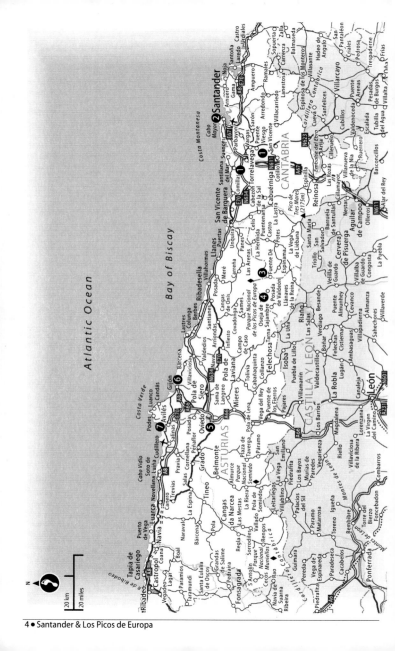

Genteel Cantabria is an island of reaction between the more radical Asturians and Basques. Historically part of Castilla, it prospered for many years as that kingdom's main sea access, and is still known as a well-heeled sort of place: "people are prone to go to puerile lengths in their vanity about heraldry", claimed writer Gregorio Marañón in the early 20th century.

Way back beyond then, from 18,000 BC onwards, a thriving Stone Age population lived in the area. They've left many remains of their culture, most notably the superb cave paintings at Altamira. These are now closed to the public, but you can see a replica of their very sophisticated art; for a more authentic atmosphere, head to one of the smaller caves in the region.

Apart from the Picos de Europa, Cantabria's principal attraction is its coast. Santander itself has some superb beaches and excellent restaurants. Santillana del Mar is misnamed (it's not on the sea ...) but is within easy reach of the sand; it's a touristed but captivating and memorable town of stone mansions and cobbled streets, while Comillas has some startling modernista architecture, including a flamboyant Gaudí building.

For such a small area, the Picos de Europa has a deservedly high reputation among visitors, who eulogize this part of the vast Cordillera Cantábrica, which is blessed with spectacular scenery, superb walking, abundant wildlife and comparatively easy access. The Picos cover the corners of three provinces: Asturias, Cantabria and León, and have a fairly mild climate due to their proximity to the sea.

Asturias is a tough, proud land that suffered greatly in the 20th century, when its radical miners were put down brutally by the army in 1934 and again in the Civil War. It is is still one of the more left-wing and egalitarian regions in Northern Spain and, along with Euskadi, in many ways its friendliest. Wherever you head in the province you're guaranteed a gruff, genuine welcome and the sound of cider corks popping.

Planning your trip

Best time to visit Santander and Los Picos de Europa

The whole of Spain is busy in July and August and, while the north isn't ridiculously crowded, you'll need to reserve rooms in advance, for which you'll be paying slightly higher prices, and significantly higher on the coast. That said, it's an enjoyable time to be in the country as there are dozens of fiestas, and everything happens outdoors. It'll be pleasantly warm on the coast and in the mountains (although you're likely to see rain in both areas), and very hot in Castilla and La Rioja – expect days in the mid to high 30s, if not higher.

June is a good time too, with milder weather and far fewer crowds, as Spanish holidays haven't started. Spring (apart from Easter week) is also quiet, and not too hot, although expect coastal showers if not serious rain. In the mountains, some routes may still be snowbound. Autumn is a good all-round time. Prices on the coast are slashed (although many hotels shut), and there are few tourists. The weather is unpredictable at this time: cool, crisp days in the mountains are likely, but on the coast you could get a week of warm sun or a fortnight of unrelenting drizzle. The cities of the interior are likely to be dry but cold.

In winter, temperatures are mild on the coast and cold inland. Accommodation is cheap, but many places in the mountains and on the coast are closed. Skiing starts in earnest in late January.

Getting to Santander and Los Picos de Europa

Air

With budget airlines having opened up several regional airports to international flights, it's easier than ever to get to Northern Spain. **Ryanair** fly to Santiago de Compostela, Valladolid, Santander, and Zaragoza from London, while **Easyjet** serve Bilbao and Asturias, **Vueling** link Bilbao, Santiago and A Coruña with London or Edinburgh, and **Air Berlin** go to Bilbao and Asturias (among others), with a connection, from many German and Austrian airports. These airlines also run routes to other European cities. Other international airlines serve Bilbao (which is connected with London, Paris, Frankfurt, and several other European cities), Vigo, Santiago de Compostela, Zaragoza and Asturias. If you're not on the budget carriers, however, it's often cheaper to fly to Madrid and connect via a domestic flight or by land transport. Madrid is a major world airport and prices tend to be competitive.

Domestic connections via Madrid or Barcelona are frequent. **Iberia** connects Madrid with most cities of the north, while **Spanair** and **Air Europa** also operate some flights. Flights are fairly expensive, with a typical Madrid–Bilbao return costing €200. There are often specials on various websites (see below) that can bring the price down considerably. If flying into Madrid from outside Spain, an onward domestic flight can often be added at little extra cost.

While budget carriers often offer excellent value (especially when booked well ahead), they offer very little flexibility. Be aware that if you're only booking a week or so in advance, it may be cheaper with other airlines such as **British Airways** or **Iberia**. Cheap fares will usually carry a heavy financial penalty for changing dates or cancellation; check the small print carefully before buying a ticket. Some airlines don't like one-way tickets; it's (ridiculously) often cheaper to buy a return.

Don't miss...

Numbers relate to map on page 4.

Before booking, it's worth doing a bit of online research. Two of the best search engines for flight comparisons are **www.kelkoo.com** and **www.kayak.com**, which compare prices from travel agencies and websites. To keep yourself up to date with the ever-changing routes of the bewildering number of budget airlines **www.whichbudget.com** is recommended. **Flightchecker** (http://flightchecker.moneysavingexpert.com) is handy for checking multiple dates for budget airline deals.

From the UK and Ireland Competition between airlines serving Spain has benefited the traveller in recent years. Budget operators have taken a significant slice of the market and forced other airlines to compete. There are several options for flying to Northern Spain from the UK and Ireland.

The cheapest direct flights are with the budget operators, whose fares can be as low as €30 return but are more usually €85-160. It's easier to get hold of a cheaper fare if you fly off-season or midweek, and if you book well in advance. The routes offered at time of writing are: **Ryanair**: London Stansted to Santiago de Compostela, Santander, Valladolid, and Zaragoza. **Easyjet**: London Stansted to Bilbao, Asturias (Oviedo/ Gijón/Avilés). **BMI**: Birmingham to Bilbao. **Aer Lingus**: Dublin to Santiago de Compostela and Bilbao. **Vueling**: London Heathrow to Bilbao and A Coruña and from Edinburgh to Santiago. Check **www. whichbudget.com** to keep apace of the changes.

Bilbao is also served from London by **Iberia** and **British Airways**. These flights often end up cheaper than **Easyjet** if you are flying at a weekend with less than a month's notice. **APEX** fares tend to be about €150-220 return and can be more economical and flexible than the budget airline if you are connecting from another British city.

Direct flights from London to Madrid are operated by **Easyjet, Ryanair, Iberia, British Airways, BMI, Air Europa, Aerolíneas Argentinas, Lufthansa** and others. **Iberia/British Airways** also connect to Madrid directly from Manchester, Edinburgh, Glasgow and Birmingham, while **Easyjet** fly to Madrid from Edinburgh, Bristol, and Liverpool, and **Spanair** from Edinburgh.

KLM, Lufthansa and **Air France** are also major carriers to Spain for those who don't mind changing at these airlines' hub airports. As well as Madrid and Barcelona these airlines all fly to Bilbao. **Iberia** and **British Airways** code share on direct flights between London and Santiago de Compostela and Oviedo/Gijón several times a week, but these flights tend to be a lot dearer; it's nearly always cheaper to connect via Madrid.

From Madrid airport (Barajas), it's very easy to hop in a taxi or the metro to the bus station (metro stop: Méndez Alvaro) or train station (Chamartín) and be in Northern Spain in a jiffy.

Iberia and Aer Lingus code share daily direct flights from Dublin to Madrid and Barcelona, while Aer Lingus runs budget flights from Dublin to Bilbao and Santiago. Ryanair operate budget flights between Dublin and London if you can find a cheap flight from the UK.

From Europe There are many direct flights from Europe to Northern Spain, but most are overpriced apart from those on budget airlines; you're often better flying in to Madrid. Budget routes to the north include **Air Berlin** services from numerous German, Austrian, and Swiss cities to Bilbao, Asturias, and Santiago de Compostela, usually via their Mallorca hub. **Ryanair** link Valladolid, Santander, and Zaragoza with European destinations such as Brussels Charleroi, Milan Bergamo, Roma Ciampino and Frankfurt Hahn. Other airlines, such as **German Wings, Brussels Airlines, Wizzair** and **Vueling**, fly a few select European routes; check www.whichbudget.com for up-to-date routes in this rapidly changing market.

On full-fare airlines, Bilbao is directly connected with several other European cities, including Frankfurt, Zürich, Brussels, Paris, Milan and Lisbon. There are flights to Madrid from most European capitals with both budget and full-fare carriers.

From North America and Canada To reach Northern Spain from across the Atlantic, the best way is to fly in via Madrid. From the east coast, flights can rise well over US$1400 in summer but, in winter or with advance purchase, you can get away with as little as US$600. Prices from the west coast are usually only US$100 or so more. **Iberia** flies direct to Madrid from many east coast cities and **British Airways** often offers reasonable add-on fares via London. A domestic extension from Madrid won't necessarily add much to the fare but it might be cheaper and/or more convenient getting the train. Flying in via other European hubs such as Paris or London is often less expensive, but adds a good few hours on to the journey. Travellers from Canada will sometimes find that it's cheaper to fly via London than Madrid.

Rail
Travelling from the UK to Northern Spain by train is unlikely to save either time or money; the only advantages lie in the pleasure of the journey itself, the chance to stop along the way, and the environmental impact of flying versus rail travel. Using **Eurostar** ① *T0870 160 6600, www.eurostar.com*, changing stations in Paris and boarding a TGV to Hendaye can have you in San Sebastián 10 hours after leaving Waterloo if the connections are kind. Once across the Channel, the trains are reasonably priced, but factor in £100-200 return on **Eurostar** and things don't look so rosy, unless you can take advantage of a special offer. Using the train/Channel ferry combination will more or less halve the cost and double the time.

The main rail gateway from the rest of Europe is Paris (Austerlitz). There's a Paris–Madrid sleeper daily, which stops at Vitoria, Burgos and Valladolid. Standard tourist class is €162/189 in a reclining seat/couchette to Madrid one-way, and proportionally less depending on where you get off. Check www.elipsos.com for specials. The cheaper option is to take a **TGV** from Paris to Hendaye, from where you can catch a Spanish train to San Sebastián and beyond.

For students, the **InterRail** pass is an attractive and cheap possibility, which can be obtained from travel agents, but note that the pass is not valid on the high-speed **AVE** or **EuroMed** trains. If you are planning the train journey, **Rail Europe** ① *T0844 484 064, www. raileurope.co.uk*, is a useful company. RENFE, Spain's rail network, has online timetables at www.renfe.es. Also see the extremely useful www.seat61.com.

Road

Bus Eurolines (www.eurolines.com) run several buses from major European cities to a variety of destinations in Northern Spain. From London, there's a bus that leaves London Victoria at 0800 on Monday and Saturday, and arrives in Bilbao at 0430 the next morning. The return leaves Bilbao at 0030 on Thursday and Saturday night, getting to London at 1945 the next evening. There's an extra bus in summer. A return fare costs about £100; it's marginally cheaper for pensioners and students, but overall isn't great value unless you're not a fan of flying. Book on T01582 404 511 or www.gobycoach.com.

Car The main route into Northern Spain is the E05/E70 tolled motorway that runs down the southwest coast of France, crossing into Spain at Irún, near San Sebastián. More scenic but slower routes cross the Pyrenees at various points. Most other motorways are free and in good condition.

Cars must be insured for third party and practically any driving licence is acceptable (but if you're from a country that a Guardia Civil would struggle to locate on a map, take an International Driving Licence). Unleaded petrol costs about €1.35 per litre in Spain.

Sea

Bear in mind that from the UK it's usually cheaper to fly and hire a car in Northern Spain than bring the motor across on the ferry. For competitive fares by sea to France and Spain, check with **Ferrysavers** ① *T0844 576 8835, www.ferrysavers.com* and **www.ferrycheap.com**, which list special offers from various operators. The website **www.seat61.com** is good for investigating train/ferry combinations.

Now that P&O no longer run a Bilbao service, the only UK-Spain ferry is the service run by **Brittany Ferries** ① *T0871 244 0744, www.brittany-ferries.co.uk*, from Plymouth and Portsmouth to Santander. There's one weekly sailing on each route, taking around 24 hours from Portsmouth and 20 hours from Plymouth. Prices are variable but can usually be found for about £70-90 each way in a reclining seat. A car adds about £150 each way, and cabins start from about £80.

At time of writing, a trial ferry service had started up between Gijón and St Nazaire in France, potentially saving a good deal of driving. See page 91 for details.

Transport in Santander and Los Picos de Europa

Public transport between the larger towns in Northern Spain is good; you can expect several buses a day between adjacent provincial capitals; these services are quick and efficient. The new network of high-speed **AVE** trains link major cities in double-quick time, but are significantly more expensive than the bus. Other train services are slow. If you want to explore much of rural Northern Spain, however, you'll probably want to hire a car, take a bike, or walk.

Rail

The Spanish national rail network **RENFE** ① *T902 240 202 (English-speaking operators), www.renfe.es*, is becoming a very useful option for getting around Northern Spain. **AVE** trains run from Madrid to Valladolid, Zaragoza and Huesca, with other routes under construction to nearly all of Northern Spain's major cities. These trains cover these large distances impressively quickly and reliably. It is an expensive but excellent service that refunds part or all of the ticket price if it arrives late. Elsewhere though, you'll find the bus is often quicker and cheaper than the train.

Prices vary significantly according to the type of service you are using. The standard fast-ish intercity service is called *Talgo*, while other intercity services are labelled *Altaria*, *Intercity*, *Diurno* and *Estrella* (overnight). Slower local trains are called *regionales*.

It's always worth buying a ticket in advance for long-distance travel, as trains are often full. The best option is to buy them via the website, which sometimes offers advance- purchase discounts. You can also book by phone, but they only accept Spanish cards. In either case, you get a reservation code, then print off your ticket at the terminals at the station. If buying your ticket at the station, allow plenty of time for queuing. Ticket windows are labelled *venta anticipada* (in advance) and *venta inmediata* (six hours or less before the journey). A better option can be to use a travel agent; the ones that sell tickets will display a **RENFE** sign, but you'll have to purchase them a day in advance. Commission is minimal.

All Spanish trains are non-smoking. The faster trains will have first-class (*preferente*) and second-class sections as well as a *cafetería*. First class costs about 30% more than standard and can be a worthwhile deal on a crowded long journey. Other pricing is bewilderingly complex. Night trains are more expensive, even if you don't take a sleeping berth, and there's a system of peak/off-peak days that makes little difference in practice. Buying a return ticket is 10-20% cheaper than two singles, but you qualify for this discount even if you buy the return leg later (but not on every service). A useful tip: if the train is 'full' for your particular destination, try to buy a ticket halfway (or even one stop), get on, and then ask the ticket inspector whether it's possible to go further. You may have to shuffle seats a couple of times, but most are fairly helpful – you can pay the excess fare on board. Don't board a train without a ticket though.

An **ISIC student card** or **under-26 card** grants a discount of between 20% to 30% on train services. If you're using a European railpass, be aware that you'll still have to make a reservation on Spanish trains and pay the small reservation fee (which covers your insurance).

The other important Northern Spanish network is **FEVE** ⓘ *www.feve.es*, whose main line runs along the north coast from Bilbao to Santander, Asturias, and as far as Ferrol in Galicia; there's another line from Bilbao to León. It's a slow line, but very picturesque. It stops at many small villages and is handy for exploring the coast. They also operate the luxury *Transcantábrico*, a week's journey along the whole network, with numerous side trips, and gourmet meals.

Both **FEVE** and **RENFE** operate short-distance *cercanías* (commuter trains) in some areas, essentially suburban train services. These are particularly helpful in Asturias and around Bilbao.

Road

Bus Buses are the staple of Spanish public transport. Services between major cities are fast, frequent, reliable and fairly cheap; the five-hour trip from Madrid to Oviedo, for example, costs €31. When buying a ticket, always check how long the journey will take, as the odd bus will be an 'all stations to' job, calling in at villages that seem surprised to even see it. *Directo* is the term for a bus that doesn't stop; it won't usually cost any more either. Various premium services (called *Supra*, *Ejecutivo* or similar) add comfort, with onboard drinks service, lounge area in the bus station and more space, but cost around 60% more.

Most cities have a single terminal, the *estación de autobuses*, which is where all short- and long-haul services leave from. Buy your tickets at the relevant window; if there isn't one, buy it from the driver. Many companies don't allow baggage in the cabin of the bus, but security is pretty good. Most tickets will have a seat number (*asiento*) on them; ask when buying the ticket if you prefer a window (*ventana*) or aisle (*pasillo*) seat. There's a huge number of intercity bus companies, some of which allow phone and online booking; the most useful in Northern Spain is **ALSA** ⓘ *T902 422 242* , *www.alsa.es*, which is based in Asturias and runs many routes. The website www.movelia.es is also useful. The platform that the bus leaves from is called a *dársena* or *andén*. If you're travelling at busy times (particularly a fiesta or national holiday) always book the bus ticket in advance. If the bus station is out of town, there are usually travel agents in the centre who can do this for you at no extra charge.

Rural bus services are slower, less frequent and more difficult to coordinate. They typically run early in the morning and late in the evening; they're designed for villagers who visit the big city once a week or so to shop.

All bus services are reduced on Sundays and, to a lesser extent, on Saturdays; some services don't run at all on weekends. Local newspapers publish a comprehensive list of departures; expect few during siesta hours. While most large villages will have at least some bus service to their provincial capital, don't expect there to be buses running to tourist attractions like monasteries, beaches or castles; it's assumed that all tourists have cars.

Most Spanish cities have their sights closely packed into the centre, so you won't find local buses particularly necessary. There's a fairly comprehensive network in most towns, though; the Ins and outs and Transport sections in this guide indicate where they come in handy. In most cities, you just board and pay the driver.

Car The roads in Northern Spain are good, excellent in many parts. While driving isn't as sedate as in parts of Northern Europe, it's generally of a very high standard, and you'll have few problems. To drive in Spain, you'll need a full driving licence from your home country. This applies to virtually all foreign nationals, but in practice, if you're from an 'unusual' country, consider an International Driving Licence or official translation of your licence into Spanish.

There are two types of motorway in Spain, *autovías* and *autopistas*; the quality of both is generally excellent, with a speed limit of 120 kph. They are signposted in blue and may have tolls payable, in which case there'll be a red warning circle on the blue sign when you're entering the motorway. An 'A' prefix to the road number indicates a motorway; an 'AP' prefix indicates a toll motorway. Tolls are generally reasonable, but extortionate in the Basque country. You can pay by cash or card. Most motorways in Northern Spain, however, are free.

Rutas Nacionales form the backbone of Spain's road network. Centrally administered, they vary wildly in quality. Typically, they are choked with traffic backed up behind trucks, and there are few stretches of dual carriageway. Driving at siesta time is a good idea if you're going to be on a busy stretch. *Rutas Nacionales* are marked with a red 'N' number. The speed limit is 100 kph outside built-up areas, as it is for secondary roads, which are numbered with a provincial prefix (eg BU-552 in Burgos province), although some are demarcated 'B' and 'C' instead.

In urban areas, the speed limit is 50 kph. Many towns and villages have sensors that will turn traffic lights red if you're over the limit on approach. City driving can be confusing, with signposting generally poor and traffic heavy; it's worth printing off the directions that your hotel may send you with a reservation. In some towns and cities, many of the hotels are officially signposted, making things easier. Larger cities may have their historic quarter blocked off by barriers: if your hotel lies within these, ring the buzzer and say the name of the hotel, and the barriers will open.

Police are increasingly enforcing speed limits in Spain, and foreign drivers are liable to a large on-the-spot fine. Drivers can also be punished for not carrying two red warning triangles to place on the road in case of breakdown, a bulb-replacement kit and a fluorescent green waistcoat to wear if you break down by the side of the road. Drink driving is being cracked down on more than was once the case; the limit is 0.5 g/l of blood, slightly less than the equivalent in the UK, for example.

Parking is a problem in nearly every town and city in Northern Spain. Red or yellow lines on the side of the street mean no parking. Blue lines indicate a metered zone, while white lines mean that some restriction is in place; a sign will give details. Parking meters can usually only be dosed up for a maximum of two hours, but they take a siesta at lunchtime too. Print the ticket off and display it in the car. Once the day's period has expired, you can charge it up for the next morning to avoid an early start. If you get a ticket, you can pay a minimal fine at the machine within the first half hour or hour instead of the full whack. Underground car parks are common and well signposted, but fairly pricey; €12-20 a day is normal. However, this is the safest option if you are going to leave any valuables in your car.

Liability insurance is required for every car driven in Spain and you must carry proof of it. If bringing your own car, check carefully with your insurers that you're covered, and get a certificate (green card). If your insurer doesn't cover you for breakdowns, consider joining the **RACE** ① *T902 120 441, www.race.es,* Spain's automobile association, which provides good breakdown cover.

Hiring a car in Spain is easy but not especially cheap. The major multinationals have offices at all large towns and airports; the company with the broadest network is **National/ATESA** ① *www.atesa.es.* Brokers, such as **Holiday Autos** ① *www.holidayautos.co.uk,* are usually cheaper than booking direct with the rental companies. Prices start at around €150 per week for a small car with unlimited mileage. You'll need a credit card and most agencies will either not accept under 25s or demand a surcharge. Rates from the airports tend to be cheaper than from towns. Before booking, use a price-comparison website like www.kelkoo.com to find the best deals.

Cycling Cycling presents a curious contrast; Spaniards are mad for the competitive sport, but comparatively uninterested in cycling as a means of transport. Thus there are plenty of cycling shops but very few bike lanes, though these are rapidly being constructed in most cities in the region. Interest in cycling is particularly high along the north coast. Contact the **Real Federación de Ciclismo en España** ① *www.rfec.com,* for more links and assistance.

Motorcycling Motorcycling is a good way to enjoy Spain and there are few difficulties to trouble the biker; bike shops and mechanics are relatively common. Hiring a motorbike, however, is difficult; there are few outlets in Northern Spain. The **Real Federación Motociclista Española** ① *www.rfme.net,* can help with links and advice.

Taxis Taxis are a good option; flagfall is €2-3 in most places (it increases slightly at night and on Sundays) and it gets you a good distance. A taxi is available if its green light is lit; hail one on the street or ask for the nearest rank (*parada de taxis*). In smaller towns or at quiet times, you'll have to ring for one. All towns have their own taxi company; phone numbers are given in the text.

Maps
The Michelin road maps are reliable for general navigation, although if you're getting off the beaten track you'll often find a local map handy. Tourist offices provide these, which vary in quality. The best topographical maps are published by the **Instituto Geográfico Nacional** (IGN). These are not necessarily more accurate than those obtainable in Britain or North America. A useful website for route planning is www.guiarepsol.com. Car hire companies have navigation systems available, though they cost a hefty supplement.

Where to stay in Santander and Los Picos de Europa

There are a reasonable number of well-equipped but characterless places on the edges or in the newer parts of towns in Spain. Similarly, chains such as NH, AC, and Hesperia have stocked Northern Spain's cities with reasonably comfortable but frequently featureless four-star business hotels. This guide has expressly minimized these in the listings, preferring to concentrate on more atmospheric options, but they are easily accessible via their websites or hotel booking brokers. If booking accommodation without this guide, always be sure to check the location if that's important to you – it's easy to find yourself a 15-minute cab ride from the town you want to be in. Having said this, the standard of accommodation in Northern Spain is very high; even the most modest of *pensiones* are usually very clean and respectable. Places to stay (*alojamientos*) are divided into three main categories; the distinctions between them follow an arcane series of regulations devised by the government.

All registered accommodations charge an 8% value-added tax (IVA); this is often included in the price at cheaper places and may be waived if you pay cash. If you have any problems, a last resort is to ask for the *libro de reclamaciones* (complaints book), an official document that, like stepping on cracks in the pavement, means uncertain but definitely horrible consequences for the hotel if anything is written in it. If you do write something in it, you have to go to the police within 24 hours and report the fact.

Hoteles, hostales and pensiones

Hoteles (marked H or HR) are graded from one to five stars and usually occupy their own building. *Hostales* (marked Hs or HsR) go from one to three stars. *Pensiones* (P) are the standard budget option, and are usually family-run flats in an apartment block. Although it's worth looking at a room before taking it, the majority are very acceptable. Spanish traditions of hospitality are alive and well; even the simplest of *pensiones* will generally provide a towel and soap, and check-out time is almost uniformly a very civilized midday. Most *pensiones* will give you keys to the exterior door; if they don't, be sure to mention the fact if you plan to stay out late.

Agroturismos and casas rurales

An excellent option if you've got transport are the networks of rural homes, called a variety of things, normally *agroturismos* or *casas rurales*. Although these are under a different classification system, the standard is often as high as any country hotel. The best of them are traditional farmhouses or old village cottages. Some are available only to rent out whole, while others operate more or less as hotels. Rates tend to be excellent compared to hotels, and many offer kitchen facilities and home-cooked meals. While many are listed in the text, there are huge numbers, especially in the coastal and mountain areas. Each regional government publishes its own listings booklet, which is available at any tourist office in the area; some of the regional tourism websites also list them. The website www.toprural.com is another good place to find them.

Albergues and refugios

There are a few youth hostels (*albergues*) around, but the accessible price of *pensiones* rarely makes it worth the trouble except for solo travellers. Spanish youth hostels are frequently populated by noisy schoolkids and have curfews and check-out times unsuitable for the late hours the locals keep. The exception is in mountain regions, where there are excellent *refugios*; simple hostels for walkers and climbers along the lines of a Scottish bothy.

Price codes

Where to stay

€€€€ over €170   **€€€** €110-170

€€ €55-110   **€** under €55

Price codes refer to a standard double/twin room, inclusive of the 8% IVA (value-added tax). The rates are for high season (usually June-August).

Restaurants

€€€ over €20   **€€** €10-20   **€** under €10

Price codes refer to the cost of a main course for one person, without a drink.

Campsites

Most campsites are set up as well-equipped holiday villages for families; many are open only in summer. While the facilities are good, they get extremely busy in peak season; the social scene is good, but sleep can be tough. They've often got playground facilities and a swimming pool; an increasing number now offer cabin or bungalow accommodation, normally a good-value option for groups or families. In other areas, camping, unless specifically prohibited, is a matter of common sense.

Food and drink in Santander and Los Picos de Europa

Nothing in Spain illustrates its differences from the rest of Europe more than its eating and drinking culture. Whether you're halfway through Sunday lunch at 1800, ordering a plate of octopus some time after midnight, snacking on *pinchos* in the street, or watching a businessman down a hefty brandy with his morning coffee, it hits you at some point that the whole of Spanish society more or less revolves around food and drink.

Eating hours are the first point of difference. Spaniards eat little for breakfast, usually just a coffee and maybe a croissant or pastry. The mid-morning coffee and piece of tortilla is a ritual, especially for office workers, and then there might be a quick bite and a drink in a bar before lunch, which is usually started between 1400 and 1530. This is the main meal of the day and the cheapest time to eat, as most restaurants offer a good-value set menu. Lunch (and dinner) is extended at weekends, particularly on Sundays, when the *sobremesa* (chatting over the remains of the meal) can go on for hours. Most folk head home for the meal during the working week and get back to work about 1700; some people have a nap (the famous siesta), some don't. It's common to have an evening drink or *tapa* in a bar after the *paseo*, if this is extended into a food crawl it's called a *tapeo*. Dinner (*cena*) is normally eaten from about 2200 onwards, although sitting down to dinner at midnight at weekends isn't unusual. In smaller towns, however, and midweek you might not get fed after 2200. Be aware that any restaurant open for dinner before 2030 could well be a tourist trap. After eating, *la marcha* (the nightlife) hits drinking bars (*bares de copas*) and then nightclubs (*discotecas*; a *club* is a brothel). Many of these places only open at weekends and are usually busiest from 0200 onwards.

Food

While the regional differences in the cuisine of Northern Spain are important, the basics remain the same. Spanish cooking relies on meat, fish/seafood, beans and potatoes given character by the chef's holy trinity: garlic, peppers and, of course, olive oil. The influence of the colonization of the Americas is evident, and the result is a hearty, filling style of meal ideally washed down with some of the nation's excellent red wines. The following is an overview of the most common dishes.

Even in areas far from the coast, the availability of good **fish and seafood** can be taken for granted. *Merluza* (hake) is the staple fish, but is pushed hard by *bacalao* (salt cod) on the north coast. A variety of farmed white fish are also increasingly popular. *Gambas* (prawns) are another common and excellent choice, backed up by a bewildering array of molluscs and crustaceans as well as numerous tasty fish. Calamari, squid and cuttlefish are common; if you can cope with the slightly slimy texture, *pulpo* (octopus) is particularly good, especially when simply boiled *a la gallega* (Galician style) and flavoured with paprika and olive oil. Supreme among the seafood are *rodaballo* (turbot) and *rape* (monkfish/anglerfish). Fresh trout from the mountain streams of Navarra or Asturias are hard to beat too; they are commonly cooked with bacon or ham (*trucha a la navarra*).

Wherever you go, you'll find cured ham (*jamón serrano*), which is always excellent, but particularly so if it's the pricey *ibérico*, taken from acorn-eating porkers in Salamanca, Extremadura and Huelva. Other cold **meats** to look out for are *cecina*, made from beef and, of course, *embutidos* (sausages), including the versatile *chorizo*. Pork is also popular as a cooked meat; its most common form is sliced loin (*lomo*). Beef is common throughout; cheaper cuts predominate, but the better steaks (*solomillo, entrecot, chuletón*) are usually superbly tender. Spaniards tend to eat them rare (*poco hecho*; ask for *al punto* for medium-rare or *bien hecho* for well done). The *chuletón* is worth a mention in its own right; a massive T-bone best taken from an ox (*de buey*) and sold by weight, which often approaches a kilogram. It's an imposing slab of meat, best shared between two or three unless you're especially peckish. *Pollo* (chicken) is common, but usually unremarkable (unless its free-range – *pollo de corral* – in which case it's superb); game birds such as *codorniz* (quail) and *perdiz* (partridge) as well as *pato* (duck) are also widely eaten. The innards of animals are popular; *callos* (tripe), *mollejas* (sweetbreads) and *morcilla* (black pudding in solid or liquid form) are all excellent, if acquired, tastes. Fans of the unusual will be keen to try *jabalí* (wild boar), *potro* (foal), *morros* (pig cheeks) and *oreja* (ear, usually from a pig or sheep).

Main dishes often come without any **accompaniments**, or chips at best. The consolation, however, is the *ensalada mixta*, whose simple name (mixed salad) often conceals a meal in itself. The ingredients vary, but it's typically a plentiful combination of lettuce, tomato, onion, olive oil, boiled eggs, asparagus, olives and tuna. The *tortilla* (a substantial potato omelette) is ever-present and often excellent. *Revueltos* (scrambled eggs), are usually tastily combined with prawns, asparagus or other goodies. Most **vegetable** dishes are based around that New World trio: the bean, the pepper and the potato. There are numerous varieties of bean in Northern Spain; they are normally served as some sort of hearty stew, often with bits of meat or seafood. *Fabada* is the Asturian classic of this variety, while *alubias con chorizo* are a standard across the region. A *cocido* is a typical mountain dish, a massive stew of chickpeas or beans with meat and vegetables; the liquid is drained off and eaten first (*sopa de cocido*). Peppers (*pimientos*), too, come in a number of forms. As well as being used to flavour dishes, they are often eaten in their own right; *pimientos rellenos* come stuffed with meat or seafood. Potatoes come as chips, *bravas* (with a garlic or spicy tomato sauce) or *a la riojana*, with chorizo and paprika. Other common vegetable dishes include *menestra* (delicious blend of cooked vegetables), which usually has some ham in it, and *ensaladilla rusa*, a tasty blend of potato, peas, peppers, carrots and mayonnaise. *Setas* (wild mushrooms) are a delight, particularly in autumn.

Desserts focus on the sweet and milky. *Flan* (a sort of crème caramel) is ubiquitous; great when *casero* (home-made), but often out of a plastic tub. *Natillas* are a similar but more liquid version, and *arroz con leche* is a cold, sweet, rice pudding typical of Northern Spain. **Cheeses** tend to be bland or salty. There are some excellent cheeses in Northern Spain, however; piquant Cabrales and Basque Idiázabal stand out.

Regional cuisine

Regional styles tend to use the same basic ingredients treated in slightly different ways, backed up by some local specialities. Asturias and Cantabria are seafood-minded on the coast but search for more warming fare in the high ground.

Eating out

One of the great pleasures of travelling in Northern Spain is eating out, but it's no fun sitting in an empty restaurant so adapt to the local hours as much as you can; it may feel strange leaving dinner until 2200, but you'll miss out on a lot of atmosphere if you don't.

The standard distinctions of bar, café and restaurant don't apply in Spain. Many places combine all three functions, and it's not always evident; the dining room (*comedor*) is often tucked away behind the bar or upstairs. *Restaurantes* are restaurants, and will usually have a dedicated dining area with set menus and à la carte options. Bars and cafés will often display food on the counter, or have a list of tapas; bars tend to be known for particular dishes they do well. Many bars, cafés and restaurants don't open on Sunday nights, and most are closed one other night a week, most commonly Monday or Tuesday.

Cafés will usually provide some kind of **breakfast** fare in the mornings; croissants and sweet pastries are the norm; freshly squeezed orange juice is also common. About 1100 they start putting out savoury fare; maybe a *tortilla*, some *ensaladilla rusa* or little ham rolls in preparation for pre-lunch snacking. It's a workers' tradition – from labourers to executives – to drop down to the local bar around 1130 for a *pincho de tortilla* (slice of potato omelette) to get them through until two.

Lunch is the biggest meal of the day for most people in Spain, and it's also the cheapest time to eat. Just about all restaurants offer a *menú del día*, which is usually a set three-course meal that includes wine or soft drink. In unglamorous workers' locals this is often as little as €8; paying anything more than €13 indicates the restaurant takes itself quite seriously. Most places open for lunch at about 1300, and stop serving at 1500 or 1530, although at weekends this can extend; it's not uncommon to see people still lunching at 1800 on a Sunday. The quality of à la carte is usually higher than the *menú*, and quantities are larger. Simpler restaurants won't offer this option except in the evenings. **Tapas** has changed in meaning over the years, and now basically refers to all bar food. This range includes free snacks given with drinks (now only standard in León and a few other places), *pinchos*, small saucer-sized plates of food (this is the true meaning of *tapa*) and more substantial dishes, usually ordered in *raciones* and designed to be shared. A *ración* in Northern Spain is no mean affair; it can often comfortably fill one person, so if you want to sample a range of things, you're better to ask for a half (*media*) or a *tapa* (smaller portion, when available).

Most restaurants open for dinner at 2030 or later. Although some places do offer a cheap set *menú*, you'll usually have to order à la carte. In quiet areas, places stop serving at 2200 on week nights, but in cities and at weekends people sit down at 2230 or later. A cheap option at all times is a *plato combinado*, most commonly offered in cafés. They're usually a greasy spoon-style mix of eggs, steak, bacon and chips or similar and are filling but rarely inspiring.

Vegetarians in Spain won't be spoiled for choice, but at least what there is tends to be good. There's a small but rapidly increasing number of dedicated vegetarian restaurants, but most other places won't have a vegetarian main course on offer, although the existence of *raciones* and salads makes this less of a burden than it might be. *Ensalada mixta* nearly always has tuna in it, but it's usually made fresh, so places will happily leave it out. *Ensaladilla rusa* is normally a good bet, but ask about the tuna too, just in case. Tortilla is simple but delicious and ubiquitous. Simple potato or pepper dishes are tasty options (although beware of peppers stuffed with meat), and many *revueltos* (scrambled eggs) are just mixed with asparagus. Annoyingly, most vegetable *menestras* are seeded with ham before cooking, and bean dishes usually contain at least some meat or animal fat. You'll have to specify *soy vegetariano/a* (I am a vegetarian), but ask what dishes contain, as ham, fish and chicken are often considered suitable vegetarian fare. Vegans will have a tougher time. What doesn't have meat nearly always contains cheese or egg.

Drink

In good Catholic fashion, **wine** is the lifeblood of Spain. It's the standard accompaniment to most meals, but also features very prominently in bars, where a glass of cheap *tinto* or *blanco* can cost as little as €0.80, although it's more normally €1.20. A bottle of house wine in a restaurant is often no more than €5 or €6. *Tinto* is red (although if you just order *vino* it's assumed that's what you want); *blanco* is white, and rosé is either *clarete* or *rosado*. A well-regulated system of *denominaciones de origen* (DO), similar to the French *appelation controlée* has lifted the reputation of Spanish wines high above the party plonk status they once enjoyed. Much of Spain's wine is produced in the north, and recent years have seen regions such as the Ribera del Duero, Rueda, Navarra, Toro, Bierzo, and Rías Baixas achieve worldwide recognition. But the daddy, of course, is still Rioja.

The overall standard of Riojas has improved markedly since the granting of the higher DOC status in 1991, with some fairly stringent testing in place. Red predominates; these are mostly medium-bodied bottles from the Tempranillo grape (with three other permitted red grapes often used to add depth or character). Whites from Viura and Malvasia are also produced: the majority of these are young, fresh and dry, unlike the traditional powerful oaky Rioja whites now on the decline. Rosés are also produced. The quality of individual Riojas varies widely according to both producer and the amount of time the wines have been aged in oak barrels and in the bottle. The words *crianza*, *reserva* and *gran reserva* refer to the length of the ageing process, while the vintage date is also given. Rioja producers store their wines at the bodega until deemed ready for drinking, so it's common to see wines dating back a decade or more on shelves and wine lists.

A growing number of people feel, however, that Spain's best reds come from further west, in the Ribera del Duero region east of Valladolid. The king's favourite tipple, Vega Sicilia, has long been Spain's most prestigious wine, but other producers from the area have also gained stellar reviews.

Visiting the area in the baking summer heat, it's hard to believe that nearby Rueda can produce quality whites, but it certainly does. Most come from the Verdejo grape and have an attractive, dry, lemony taste; Sauvignon Blanc has also been planted with some success.

Galicia produces some excellent whites too; the coastal Albariño vineyards produce a sought-after dry wine with a very distinctive bouquet. Ribeiro is another good Galician white, and the reds from there are also tasty, having some similarity to those produced in nearby northern Portugal. Ribeira Sacra is another inland Galician denomination producing whites and reds from a wide range of varietals.

Among other regions, Navarra, long known only for rosé, is producing some quality red wines unfettered by the stricter rules governing production in Rioja, while Bierzo, in western León province, also produces interesting wines from the red Prieto Picudo and Mencía grapes. Other DO wines in Northern Spain include Somontano, a red and white appelation from Aragón and Toro, whose baking climate makes for full-bodied reds. Some Toro wines have achieved a very high worldwide profile.

An unusual wine worth trying is *txakolí*, with a small production on the Basque coast. The most common is a young, refreshing, acidic white which has a green tinge and slight sparkle, often accentuated by pouring from a height. The best examples, from around Getaria, go well with seafood. The wine is made from under-ripe grapes of the Ondarrubi Zuria variety; there's a less common red species and some rosé.

One of the joys of Spain, though, is the rest of the wine. Order a *menú del día* at a cheap restaurant and you'll be unceremoniously served a cheap bottle of local red (sometimes without even asking for it). Wine snobbery can leave by the back door at this point: it may be cold, but you'll find it refreshing; it may be acidic, but once the olive-oil laden food arrives, you'll be glad of it. It's not there to be judged, it's a staple like bread and, like bread, it's sometimes excellent, it's sometimes bad, but mostly it fulfils its purpose perfectly. Wine is not a luxury item in Spain, so people add water to it if they feel like it, or lemonade (*gaseosa*), or *cola* (to make the party drink called *calimocho*). Tinto de verano is a summer slurper similar to sangría, a mixture of red wine, gaseosa, ice, and optional fruit.

Spanish **beer** is mostly lager, usually reasonably strong, fairly gassy, cold and good. On the tapas trail, many people order *cortos* (*zuritos* in the Basque lands), usually about 100 ml. A *caña* is a larger draught beer, usually about 200 ml. Order a *cerveza* and you'll get a bottled beer. Many people order their beer *con gas*, topped up with mineral water, sometimes called a *clara*, although this normally means it's topped with lemonade. In some pubs, particularly those specializing in different beers (*cervecerías*), you can order pints (*pintas*).

Cider (*sidra*) is an institution in Asturias. The cider is flat, sour and yeasty; the appley taste will be a surprise after most commercial versions of the drink. Asturias' *sidrerías* offer some of Spain's most enjoyable bar life, see box, page 106, with excellent food, a distinctive odour, sawdust on the floor, and the cider poured from above head height by uniformed waiters to give it some bounce.

Spirits are cheap in Spain. Vermouth (*vermut*) is a popular pre-lunch *aperitif*, as is *patxarán*. Many bars make their own vermouth by adding various herbs and fruits and letting it sit in barrels; this can be excellent, particularly if its from a *solera*. This is a system where liquid is drawn from the oldest of a series of barrels, which is then topped up with the next oldest, resulting in a very mellow characterful drink. After dinner or lunch it's time for a *copa*: people relax over a whisky or a brandy, or hit the mixed drinks (*cubatas*): *gin tonic* is obvious, as is *vodka con cola*. Spirits are free-poured and large; don't be surprised at a 100 ml measure. A mixed drink costs €3.50-6. Whisky is popular, and most bars have a good range. Spanish brandy is good, although its oaky vanilla flavours don't appeal to everyone. There are numerous varieties of rum and flavoured liqueurs. When ordering a spirit, you'll be expected to choose which brand you want; the local varieties (eg *Larios* gin, *DYC* whisky) are marginally cheaper than their imported brethren but lower in quality. *Chupitos* are shots; restaurants will often throw in a free one at the end of a meal, or give you a bottle of *orujo* (grape spirit) to pep up your black coffee.

Juice is normally bottled and expensive; *mosto* (grape juice; really pre-fermented wine) is a cheaper and popular soft drink in bars. There's the usual range of **fizzy drinks** (*gaseosas*) available. *Horchata* is a summer drink, a sort of milkshake made from tiger nuts.

Water (*agua*) comes *con* (with) or *sin* (without) *gas*. The tap water is totally safe to drink, but it's not always the nicest; many Spaniards drink bottled water at home.

Coffee (*café*) is usually excellent and strong. *Solo* is black, mostly served espresso style. Order *americano* if you want a long black, *cortado* if you want a dash of milk, or *con leche* for about half milk. A *carajillo* is a coffee with brandy. **Tea** (*té*) is served without milk unless you ask; herbal teas (*infusiones*) are common, especially chamomile (*manzanilla*) and mint (*menta poleo*). **Chocolate** is a reasonably popular drink at breakfast time or in the afternoon (*merienda*), served with *churros*, fried doughsticks that seduce about a quarter of visitors and repel the rest.

Festivals in Santander and Los Picos de Europa

Even the smallest village in Spain has a fiesta, and some have several. Although mostly nominally religious in nature, they usually include the works; a mass and procession or two to be sure, but also live music, bullfights, competitions, fireworks and copious drinking of *calimocho*, a mix of red wine and cola (not as bad as it sounds). A feature of many are the *gigantes y cabezudos*, huge-headed papier-mâché figures based on historical personages who parade the streets. Adding to the sense of fun are *peñas*, boisterous social clubs who patrol the streets making music, get rowdy at the bullfights and drink wine all night and day. Most fiestas are in summer, and if you're spending much time in Spain in that period you're bound to run into one; expect some trouble finding accommodation. Details of the major town fiestas can be found in the travel text. National holidays and long weekends (*puentes*) can be difficult times to travel; it's important to reserve tickets in advance. If the holiday falls mid-week, it's usual form to take an extra day off, forming a long weekend known as a *puente* (bridge).

Public holidays

The holidays listed here are national or across much of Northern Spain; local fiestas and holidays are detailed in the main text. These can be difficult times to travel; it's important to reserve travel in advance to avoid queues and lack of seats.

1 Jan Año Nuevo, New Year's Day.
6 Jan Reyes Magos/Epifanía, Epiphany; when Christmas presents are given.
Easter Jueves Santo, Viernes Santo, Día de Pascua (Maundy Thu, Good Fri, Easter Sun).

1 May Fiesta de Trabajo, Labour Day.
28 Jul Día Nacional de Cantabria.
15 Aug Asunción, Feast of the Assumption.
12 Oct Día de la Hispanidad, Spanish National Day (Columbus Day, Feast of the Virgin of the Pillar).
1 Nov Todos los Santos, All Saints' Day.
6 Dec El Día de la Constitución Española, Constitution Day.
8 Dec Inmaculada Concepción, Feast of the Immaculate Conception.
25 Dec Navidad, Christmas Day.

Essentials A-Z

Accident and emergency
There are various emergency numbers, but the general one across the nation is now T112. This will get you the police, ambulance, or fire brigade. T091 gets just the police.

Children
Kids are kings in Spain, and it's one of the easiest places to take them along on holiday. Children socialize with their parents from an early age here, and you'll see them eating in restaurants and out in bars well after midnight. The outdoor summer life and high pedestrianization of the cities is especially suitable and stress-free for both you and the kids to enjoy the experience.

Spaniards are friendly and accommodating towards children, and you'll undoubtedly get treated better with them than without, except perhaps in the most expensive restaurants and hotels. Few places, however, are equipped with highchairs, unbreakable plates or baby-changing facilities. Children are expected to eat the same food as their parents, although you'll sometimes see a *menú infantil* at a restaurant, which typically has simpler dishes and smaller portions.

The cut-off age for children paying half or no admission/passage on public transport and in tourist attractions varies widely. **RENFE** trains let children under 4 travel for free, and its discount passage of around 50% applies up to the age of 12. Most car rental companies have child seats available, but it's wise to book these in advance.

As for attractions, beaches are an obvious highlight, but many of the newer museums are hands-on, and playgrounds and parks are common. Campsites cater to families and the larger ones often have child-minding facilities and activities.

Customs and duty free
Non-EU citizens are allowed to import 1 litre of spirits, 2 litres of wine and 200 cigarettes or 250 g of tobacco or 50 cigars. EU citizens are theoretically limited by personal use only though individual countries may specify what they regard this as being.

Electricity
Spain uses the standard European 220V plug, with 2 round pins.

Health
Health for travellers in Spain is rarely a problem. Medical facilities are good, and the worst most travellers experience is an upset stomach, usually merely a result of the different diet rather than any bug.

The water is safe to drink, but isn't always that pleasant, so many travellers (and locals) stick to bottled water. The sun in Spain can be harsh, so take adequate precautions to prevent heat exhaustion/sunburn. Many medications that require a prescription in other countries are available over the counter at pharmacies in Spain. Pharmacists are highly trained but don't necessarily speak English. In all medium-sized towns and cities, at least one pharmacy is open 24 hrs; this is organized on a rota system; details are posted in the window of all pharmacies and in local newspapers.

Insurance
British and other European citizens should get hold of a **European Health Insurance Card** (**EHIC**), available via www.dh.gov. uk or from post offices in the UK, before leaving home. This guarantees free medical care throughout the EU. Other citizens should seriously consider medical insurance, but check for reciprocal Spanish cover with your private or public health scheme first.

Insurance is a good idea anyway to cover you for theft, etc. In the event of theft, you'll have to make a report at the local police station within 24 hrs and obtain a report to show your insurers. (English levels at the police station are likely to be low, so try to take a Spanish speaker with you to help).

Language

For travelling purposes, everyone in Northern Spain speaks Spanish, known either as *castellano* or *español*, and it's a huge help to know some. Most young people know some English, and standards are rapidly rising, but don't assume that people aged 40 or over know any at all. Spaniards are often shy to attempt to speak English. While many visitor attractions have some sort of information available in English (and to a lesser extent French and German), many don't, or have English tours only in times of high demand. Most tourist office staff will speak at least some English, and there's a good range of translated information available in most places.

While efforts to speak the language are appreciated, it's more or less expected, to the same degree as English is expected in Britain or the USA. Nobody will be rude if you don't speak any Spanish, but nobody will think to slow their rapidfire stream of the language for your benefit either, or pat you on the back for producing a few phrases in their tongue.

The other languages you'll come across in Northern Spain are *Euskara/Euskera* (the Basque language), *Galego* (Galician), *Bable* (the Asturian dialect) and perhaps *Aragonés* (Aragonese).

Money

Check www.xe.com for exchange rates.

Currency

In 2002, Spain switched to the euro, bidding farewell to the peseta. The euro (€) is divided into 100 *céntimos*. Euro notes are standard across the whole zone, and come in denominations of 5, 10, 20, 50, 100, and the rarely seen 200 and 500. Coins have one standard face and one national face; all coins are, however, acceptable in all countries. The coins are slightly difficult to tell apart when you're not used to them. The coppers are 1, 2 and 5 cent pieces, the golds are 10, 20 and 50, and the silver/gold combinations are €1 and €2. The exchange rate at the switchover was approximately €6 to 1000 pesetas or 166 pesetas to the euro. So if someone says they paid *cien mil*, they probably mean 100,000 pesetas; €600. People still tend to think in pesetas when talking about large amounts like house prices.

ATMs and banks

The best way to get money in Spain is by plastic. ATMs are plentiful in Spain, and just about all of them accept all the major international debit and credit cards. The Spanish bank won't charge for the transaction, though they will charge a mark-up on the exchange rate, but beware of your own bank hitting you for a hefty fee: check with them before leaving home. Even if they do, it's likely to be a better deal than exchanging cash. The website www.moneysavingexpert.com has a good rundown on the most economical ways of accessing cash while travelling.

Banks are usually open Mon-Fri 0830-1400 (and Sat in winter) and many change foreign money (sometimes only the central branch in a town will do it). Commission rates vary widely; it's usually best to change large amounts, as there's often a minimum commission of €6 or so. Nevertheless, banks nearly always give better rates than change offices (*casas de cambio*), which are fewer by the day. If you're stuck outside banking hours, some large department stores such as the *Corte Inglés* change money at knavish rates. Traveller's cheques are accepted in many shops, although they are far less common than they were.

Tax

Nearly all goods and services in Spain are subject to a value-added tax (IVA). This is only 8% for most things the traveller will encounter, including food and hotels, but is as high as 18% on some things. IVA is normally included in the stated prices. You're technically entitled to claim it back if you're a non-EU citizen, for purchases over €90. If you're buying something pricey, make sure you get a stamped receipt clearly showing the IVA component, as well as your name and passport number; you can claim the amount back at major airports on departure. Some shops will have a form to smooth the process.

Cost of living and travelling

Prices have soared since the euro was introduced; some basics rose by 50-80% in 3 years, and hotel and restaurant prices can even seem dear by Western European standards these days. Spain's average monthly salary of €1300 is low by EU standards, and the minimum monthly salary of €600 is very low indeed.

Spain can still be a reasonably cheap place to travel if you're prepared to forgo a few luxuries. If you're travelling as a pair, staying in cheap *pensiones*, eating a set meal at lunchtime, travelling short distances by bus or train daily, and snacking on tapas in the evenings, €65 per person per day is reasonable. If you camp and grab picnic lunches from shops, you could reduce this considerably. In a cheap hotel or good *hostal* and using a car, €130 each a day and you'll not be counting pennies; €250 per day and you'll be very comfy indeed unless you're staying in 4- or 5-star accommodation.

Accommodation is more expensive in summer than in winter, particularly on the coast. The news isn't great for the solo traveller; single rooms tend not to be particularly good value, and they are in short supply. Prices range from 60%

to 80% of the double/twin price; some establishments even charge the full rate. If you're going to be staying in 3- to 5-star hotels, booking them ahead on internet discount sites can save a lot of money.

Public transport is generally cheap; intercity bus services are quick and low-priced and trains are reasonable, though the fast AVE trains cost substantially more.

Petrol is relatively cheap: standard unleaded petrol is around €1.35 per litre and diesel around €1.30. In some places, particularly in tourist areas, you may be charged up to 20% more to sit outside a restaurant. It's also worth checking if the 8% IVA (sales tax) is included in menu prices, especially in the more expensive restaurants; it should say on the menu whether this is the case.

Post

The Spanish post is notoriously inefficient and slow by European standards. Post offices (*correos*) generally open Mon-Fri 0800-1300, 1700-2000; Sat 0800-1300, although main offices in large towns stay open all day. Stamps can be bought here or at tobacconists (*estancos*). A letter or postcard within Spain costs €0.39, within Europe €1.07, and elsewhere €1.38.

Safety

Northern Spain is generally a very safe place. While port cities like Bilbao, Vigo and Santander have some dodgy areas, tourist crime is very low in this region, and you're more likely to have something returned (that you left on that train) than something stolen. That said, don't invite crime by leaving luggage or cash in cars. If parking in a city or, particularly, a popular hiking zone, try to make it clear there's nothing to nick inside by opening the glovebox, etc. Muggings are very rare, but don't leave bags unattended.

There are several types of police, helpful enough in normal circumstances. The paramilitary **Guardia Civil** dress in green and are responsible for the roads (including speed traps and the like), borders and law enforcement away from towns. They're not a bunch to get the wrong side of but are polite to tourists and have thankfully lost the bizarre winged hats they used to sport. The **Policía Nacional** are responsible for most urban crimefighting. Brown-shirted folk, these are the ones to go to if you need to report anything stolen, etc. **Policía Local/Municipal** are present in large towns and cities and are responsible for some urban crime, as well as traffic control and parking.

Telephone → *Country code +34.*

There's a public telephone in many bars, but hearing the conversation over the ambient noise can be a hard task and rates are slightly higher than on the street. Phone booths on the street are mostly operated by **Telefónica**, and all have international direct dialling (00 is the prefix for international calls). They accept coins from €0.05 upwards and phone cards, which can be bought from *estancos*.

For directory enquiries, dial T11818 for national or T11825 for international numbers. The local operator is on T1009 and the international one on T1008.

Domestic landlines have 9-digit numbers beginning with 9 (occasionally with 8). Although the first 3 digits indicate the province, you have to dial the full number from wherever you are calling, including abroad. Mobiles numbers start with 6.

Mobiles (*móviles*) are big in Spain and coverage is very good. Most foreign mobiles will work in Spain (although older North American ones won't); check with your service provider about what the call costs will be like. Many mobile networks require you to call up before leaving your home country to activate overseas service ('roaming'). If you're staying a while, it may be cheaper to buy a Spanish mobile or SIM card, as there are always numerous offers and discounts.

Time

Spain operates on western European time, ie GMT +1, and changes its clocks in line with the rest of the EU.

'Spanish time' isn't as elastic as it used to be, but if you're told something will happen *'enseguida'* ('straight away') it may take 10 mins, if you're told *'cinco minutos'* (5 mins), grab a seat and a book. Transport, especially buses, leaves promptly.

Tipping

Tipping in Spain is far from compulsory, but much practised. Around 10% is considered extremely generous in a restaurant; 3-5% is more usual. It's rare for a service charge to be added to a bill. Waiters do not normally expect tips for lunchtime set meals or tapas, but here and in bars and cafés people will often leave small change, especially for table service. Taxi drivers don't expect a tip, but will be pleased to receive one. In rural areas, churches will often have a local keyholder who will open it up for you; if there's no admission charge, a tip or donation is appropriate (say €1 per head; more if they've given a detailed tour).

Tourist information

The tourist information infrastructure in Northern Spain is organized by the regional governments and is generally excellent, with a wide range of information, often in English, German and French as well as Spanish. Offices within the region can provide maps of the area and towns, and lists of registered accommodation, usually with 1 booklet for hotels, *hostales*, and *pensiones*; another for campsites, and another, especially worth picking up, listing farmstay and rural accommodation, which has taken off in a big way; hundreds are added yearly. Opening hours are longer in major cities; many rural offices are only open in summer. Average opening hours are Mon-Sat 1000-1400, 1600-1900, Sun 1000-1400. Offices are often closed on Sun or Mon. Staff often speak English and other European languages and are well trained. The offices (*oficinas de turismo*) are often signposted to some degree within the town or city. Staff may ask where you are from; this is not nosiness but for statistical purposes.

The regional tourist boards of Northern Spain have useful websites, the better of which have extensive accommodation, restaurant, and sights listings. You can usually order brochures online too. They are:
Asturias, www.asturias.es
Cantabria, www.turismodecantabria.com

Other useful websites
http://maps.google.es Street maps of most Spanish towns and cities.
www.alsa.es Northern Spain's major bus operator. Book online.
www.bilbao.net The city's excellent website.
www.cyberspain.com Good background on culture and fiestas.
www.dgt.es The transport department website has up-to-date information in Spanish on road conditions throughout the country. Useful for snowy winters.
www.elpais.es Online edition of Spain's biggest-selling non-sports daily paper. English edition available.
www.feve.es Website of the coastal FEVE train service.
www.guiarepsol.com Excellent online route planner for Spanish roads, also available in English.
www.idealspain.com A good source of practical information about the country designed for people relocating there.
www.inm.es Site of the national metereological institute, with the day's weather and next-day forecasts.
www.movelia.es Online timetables and ticketing for several bus companies.
www.paginasamarillas.es Yellow Pages.
www.paginasblancas.es White Pages.

www.parador.es Parador information, including locations, prices and photos.
www.red2000.com A good introduction to Spanish geography and culture, with listings.
www.renfe.es Online timetables and tickets for RENFE train network.
www.soccer-spain.com A website in English dedicated to Spanish football.
www.spain.info The official website of the Spanish tourist board.
www.ticketmaster.es Spain's biggest ticketing agency for concerts, etc, with online purchase.
www.todoturismorural.com and **www.toprural.com** 2 excellent sites for *casas rurales*.
www.tourspain.es A useful website run by the Spanish tourist board.
www.typicallyspanish.com News and links on all things Spanish.

Visas
Entry requirements are subject to change, so always check with the Spanish tourist board or an embassy/consulate if you're not an EU citizen. EU citizens and those from countries within the Schengen agreement can enter Spain freely. UK/Irish citizens will need to carry a passport, while an identity card suffices for other EU/Schengen nationals. Citizens of Australia, the USA, Canada, New Zealand and Israel can enter without a visa for up to 90 days. Other citizens will require a visa, obtainable from Spanish consulates or embassies. These are usually issued very quickly and valid for all Schengen countries. The basic visa is valid for 90 days, and you'll need 2 passport photos, proof of funds covering your stay and possibly evidence of medical cover (ie insurance). For extensions of visas, apply to an *oficina de extranjeros* in a major city.

Contents

Santander & the coast of Cantabria

Santander and around

Still an important Spanish port, Santander has for years encouraged visitors to turn their attentions away from its industrial side and towards its series of superb beaches. These gird the barrio of Sardinero, which became a genteel and exclusive resort for the summering upper classes from the mid-19th century on. An earthier lifestyle can be found around the old centre, which has an excellent collection of restaurants and bars, where old wine bodegas have been converted into some of Northern Spain's best tapas venues. Santander's ferry link to Britain makes it many visitors' first point of entry into Spain; it's a relaxing and pleasant introduction to the country, which pleases more for its ambience and seaside than any cultural highlights.

Inland Cantabria is still very rural; mulecarts and cow traffic jams are still a common sight once off the main roads. The main road routes forge south to Palencia and Burgos respectively through attractive countryside. The principal towns in the area, Torrelavega and Reinosa, are both depressing and dull industrial centres, but there are enough small attractions to make a trip in the area interesting.

The eastern Cantabrian coast is a fairly uncomplicated place, with decent beaches and a sprinkling of resorts and fishing towns that attract many summer visitors from Madrid and the Basque lands. The nicest place by far is Castro Urdiales, while the large beach town of Laredo offers a great stretch of sand, a pretty centre, watersports and good sunny season nightlife. Smaller villages, such as Escalante, offer an inviting slice of rural Cantabria, but other sections of the coast between Santander and Laredo are blighted by ugly development.

Arriving in Santander → *Phone code: 942. Population:182,700.*

Getting there Santander is connected by bus and train with the rest of Northern Spain, and by plane domestically with Madrid and Barcelona, and internationally by **Ryanair** with London Stansted and Dublin among other European airports. It's linked by ferry from the centre of town to Plymouth and Portsmouth, operated by **Brittany Ferries**. ▸ *See Transport, page 38.*

Getting around Santander is long and thin, with its beaches a good couple of kilometres from its old centre. Fortunately, buses are very frequent, with nearly all lines plying the waterside. Taxis are fairly prevalent too; a fare from Sardinero to the centre won't cost much more than €4-5.

Best time to visit August is the best time to visit Santander, with the International Festival in full swing and superb weather guaranteed. The downside is the number of sunseekers, and the difficulty of finding accommodation, which increases in price. The sea is pretty chilly, so if you're not here to swim, April and May should offer decent warm weather and not too much rain; apart from Easter week, the accommodation is a bargain outside the summer months.

Tourist information and tours The main **Cantabrian tourist office** ⓘ *T942 310 708, ofitur@cantabria.org, daily 0930-1330, 1600-1900,* is in the Mercado del Este building in the centre of town. They also run information kiosks at the ferry terminal and airport that are open to coincide with arrivals. There is a **municipal office** ⓘ *T942 203 000, turismo@ ayto-santander.es, mid-Jun to mid-Sep daily 0900-2100, mid-Sep to Mar Mon-Fri 0900-1900, Sat 1000-1400, Apr to mid-Jun Mon-Fri 0830-1900, Sat and Sun 1000-1900,* near the ferry terminal in the Jardines de Pereda park, as well as a **summer-only office** at the beach in Sardinero. A **tourist bus** ⓘ *www.santandertour.com,* plies a circular route around the town and its beaches, with information and a 'hop-on hop-off' system. Tickets and schedules are available at the tourist office in the Jardines de Pereda.

From the Calderón jetty on the Paseo de Pereda, **passenger ferries** ⓘ *T942 211 753, www.losreginas.com, single/return €2.30/4.30,* run across the bay to **Pedreña** (famous as the hometown of golfer Severiano Ballesteros) and **Somo**, from where you can walk along the extensive El Puntal beach. These are great boat trips on a pleasant day; in summer there are also circular boat trips of an hour (€9) or 2½ hours (€11.50).

Background

As the Reconquista progressed and the Moors were driven southwards, the north coast became increasingly important as an export point for Castilian produce from the expanding interior. The northern ports joined together in 1296 to form the **Hermandad de las Marismas**, a trading union that included Santander and nearby Laredo along with La Coruña and San Sebastián. Although Laredo was a more important port for much of Spain's Imperial period, Britain's Charles I picked Santander to sail home from after his incredible jaunt through France to Madrid in 1623.

Santander's major growth period as a port came in the 19th century; this was also the time that it achieved fashionable status as a resort, which it has retained. Despite the aristocratic feel of parts of the town, Santander was firmly in the Republican camp during the Civil War but finally fell in August 1937. Much of the town centre was destroyed in a

which originated in the Archbishop's palace. The Franco years didn't treat
badly, though. So much so that a statue of the *caudillo* himself on horseback
the town hall right until the last days of 2008, when he finally rode off into
nsidered to be a potential embarrassment to Santander's bid to be a 2016
Capital of Culture. The fascist street names remain in place, though.

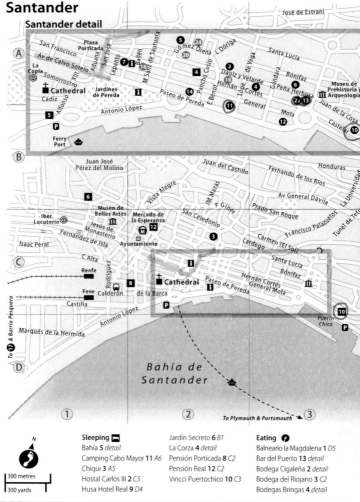

Santander
Santander detail

Sleeping 🛏		Eating 🍴
Bahía 5 *detail*	Jardín Secreto 6 *B1*	Balneario la Magdalena 1 *D5*
Camping Cabo Mayor 11 *A6*	La Corza 4 *detail*	Bar del Puerto 13 *detail*
Chiqui 3 *A5*	Pensión Porticada 8 *C2*	Bodega Cigaleña 2 *detail*
Hostal Carlos III 2 *C5*	Pensión Real 12 *C2*	Bodega del Riojano 3 *C2*
Husa Hotel Real 9 *D4*	Vincci Puertochico 10 *C3*	Bodegas Bringas 4 *detail*

300 metres
300 yards

Places in Santander

Santander doesn't possess a wealth of historical buildings; the principal attraction is its picturesque shoreline, including excellent town beaches east of the centre. In the centre, the **cathedral** ① *Mon-Fri 1000-1300, 1600-2000, Sat 1000-1300, 1630-2000, Sun 1000-1330, 1700-2100*, is reasonably interesting. Largely destroyed by the 1941 fire, its church is dull,

although the cloister offers a chance to relax from the street for a moment. The **crypt** ① *0800-1300, 1700-2000 (1600-2000 summer)*, around the back, is used for Masses, and is an intriguing little space, with curious stubby columns and ill-lit Roman ruins. A reliquary holds the silver-plated heads of San Emeterio and San Celedonio, the city patrons.

Nearby, the Ayuntamiento is backed by the excellent **Mercado de la Esperanza** with lashings of fruit, fish, meat and deli products; the place to buy your hams and olive oils if you're heading back home on the ferry.

Not far from here is the **Museo de Bellas Artes** ① *C Rubio 5, T942 239 485, Mon-Fri 1015-1300, 1730-2000, Sat 1000-1300; opens 30 mins later in summer; free*, a fairly mediocre collection. The highlight is many of Goya's *Horrors of War* prints, a dark and haunted series; there's also a portrait of Fernando VII, which isn't one of his better works. A small Miró is also notable, as are several sculptures by the late Basque, Jorge Oteiza, among them an expressive *Adam and Eve*.

The **Museo Marítimo** ① *C San Martín de Bajamar s/n, T942 274 962, Oct-Apr Tue-Sun 1000-1800, May-Sep Tue-Sun 1000-1930, €6*, on the waterfront, celebrates the city's fishing heritage, with good displays on navigation and boat building as well as a whale skeleton and some live fish and molluscs in tanks. There's a restaurant here with a good *menú del día*, which you can eat with great views of the bay.

The **Museo de Prehistoria y Arqueología** houses a collection of well-presented pieces from the province's past, many of which are creations of Neanderthal and modern man, and were found in several caves around the region. It was closed pending a move to a new location at time of research; check with the tourist office.

The **waterfront** is the nicest part of this area; it fills with people during the *paseo* and there's also a bike lane. Behind it the narrow streets are filled with tapas bars, small art galleries, and antique shops. The **Puerto Chico** is the leisure marina; after passing this you come to the huge festival centre; quite attractive when floodlit, less winning by day.

The beaches

Past the festival centre, Avenida de la Reina Victoria heads for the sands past a millionaire's row of very upmarket houses (some of Northern Spain's most expensive residences).

The **Península de la Magdalena** protects the bay of Santander from the Atlantic and is topped by a flashy *palacio*. This was a gift from the city to the king but it now houses the renowned summer university that draws people from around the globe. Jan Morris described the building as 'like a child's idea of a palace, surrounded on three sides by the sea and on the fourth by loyal subjects'. A small **zoo** nearby holds marine animals.

On the bay side of the peninsula are a couple of pretty beaches, **Playa de la Magdalena** and **Playa de los Bikinis**; just around on the sea side is the artificial **Playa del Camello**, named for the humped rock that sticks out of the water opposite it.

Sardinero is the centre of the sand suburbs; an attractively unmodern collection of belle époque buildings that back two superb beaches named **La Primera** and **La Segunda**. The Primera is the beach to be seen at; it's backed by the elegantly restored casino and several pricey hotels. The Segunda is less crowded and usually gets better waves, either at the far end or around the spur that divides the two. Both are kept creditably clean and have enough sand that you're never hurdling bodies to reach the water. Sardinero can be reached by bus Nos 1, 2, 3, 4, 7, or 15 from the waterfront in the centre of town.

From the end of the Segunda beach, a coastal path begins that skirts a golf course around the Cabo Menor headland before reaching the **Mataleñas** beach (also accessible by car) and eventually the Cabo Mayor lighthouse.

Moving further west, the great beaches continue. Some of the best are around **Liencres**, some 12 km from the centre of Santander. The main strand here is the double beach of Valdearenas: the kiosk on the smaller of the two does great rabas for a seaside snack. There are some surfable waves here, and the beach is backed by a pretty *parque natural* of dunes. Nearby, **Arnia** and **Covachas** are other pretty beachy bays; Arnia has a bar-restaurant with great views.

South of Santander → For listings, see pages 33-39.

Puente Viesgo, 30 km south of Santander, is a peaceful spa village long used as a weekend retreat from Santander but of great interest because of the caves up on the hill above, 1.5 km from town and one of the highlights of the province.

Cuevas del Castillo

ⓘ *T942 598 425, May-Sep daily 1000-1300, 1600-1930; Oct-Apr Wed-Sun 0930-1555; entry is by guided tour in Spanish, but the guides speak very clearly and slowly and make every effort to be understood. €3; tours run roughly every hour and last 45 mins; daily visitors have a maximum limit; it's worth booking in summer and also in winter to avoid the lengthy wait for a group to form.*

The Cuevas del Castillo were home to thousands of generations of Neanderthal man and Cro-Magnon man (Homo sapiens); with the earliest occupation being dated at some 130,000 years ago. Both left extensive remains of tools and weapons (Teilhard de Chardin and Albert of Monaco both got their hands dirty in the excavations here), but Cro-Magnon man did some decorating in a series of paintings that extend deep into the cave complex; these were discovered in 1903. The earliest efforts date from around 30,000 years ago and some are of several outlines of hands, created with red ochre. Interestingly, most of the prints found are of the left hand, suggesting that most folk were right-handed even back then. More sophisticated works are from later but still predate the more advanced work at Altamira. There are outlines of bison here too, as well as deer, and a long series of discs that has mystified theorists.

Although the quality of the art is nothing to touch Altamira, it's a much more satisfying experience to see the originals here than the replicas. It's atmospheric too, for the caves are fantastic; the one open for visits is a sort of Gothic cathedral in lime.

The tourist board of Cantabria produce an excellent booklet, *Patrimonio Paleolítico*, in Spanish but with clear details and well illustrated, detailing a number of other caves in the area with Palaeolithic art.

Liérganes

Picturesquely set alongside a lively burbling river, this sweet village makes a fine day trip from Santander or a peaceful overnight stop for a couple of days. Its centre is a blend of noble baroque stone mansions and turn-of-the-20th-century *indiano* dwellings, all sensitively restored. It's a popular summer retreat for wealthy Cantabrians, and has several intriguing *posadas* to stay in.

There's a small **tourist kiosk** ⓘ *T942 528 021, aytolierganes@aytolierganes.es, summer Mon-Fri 1000-2000, winter Mon, Wed-Fri 1000-1500*, by the river that will give you a map of the town and can also advise about various marked walks in the verdant valley and surrounding hills.

Liérganes can be reached on regular **FEVE** *cercanía* trains from Santander. In a car, head along the A-8 motorway towards Bilbao from Santander, and take the Torrelavega turn off just after the Solares exit.

Santoña and Escalante

Around the headland from Laredo, Santoña is a fishing town famous throughout Spain for its anchovies, which have DO (*denominación de origin*) status. Just 6 km short of it, the village of Escalante is redolent of past glories with its noble stone buildings kitted out with gnarled wooden balconies and *soportales* (ground floor wooden colonnades). It's a great spot to hole up for a couple of days and a really appealing slice of rural Cantabria, set on the edge of a wetland reserve with good birdwatching opportunities. On the western side of town, the solid parish church is set on the edge of green fields; a sizeable nearby monastery is another of several notable edifices.

Laredo

Part of the *Hermandad de las Marismas* (brotherhood of sea towns), Laredo was once an important port and the place from where Juana La Loca set sail in a fleet of 120 ships to her arranged marriage in Flanders; an ill-starred alliance that led to her complete mental breakdown. Her son Carlos V used the port too, to return to Spain weary and old, on his way to retirement and a peaceful death at the monastery of Yuste. In earlier times, Laredo was a big Roman seaport, named Portus Luliobrigensium, scene of a major naval engagement.

Laredo still nurses a handful of small fishing smacks in its harbour, but the town's sole focus these days is tourism, powered by its sunny climate and superb beach, **La Salvé**, 5 km of golden sand arcing round the bay. It's a big town, and there are kilometres of ugly resort housing along the beach; if you're prepared for that, it's a likeable place, particularly if you spend some time in its compact old town. It's worth visiting the 13th-century **Iglesia de San Francisco**, as well as sniffing out a tunnel carved in the 1860s that makes its way through the headland to a small harbour. Otherwise, relax on the sand and prepare for the lively summer nightlife. There's a cheerfully efficient **tourist office** ① *T942 611 096, daily 0930-1330, 1600-1900*, in the Alameda Miramar park.

Castro Urdiales and around

Eastern Cantabria's nicest town, Castro Urdiales is a good-humoured seaside place with just the right mixture of resort and original character to make it attractive. The coastline here has the Basque rockiness and Castro is still an important fishing port (famous for anchovies) with a big harbour and staunch nautical feel. The **tourist office** ① *Av de la Constitución, daily 0930-1330, 1600-1900*, is on the waterfront.

The **waterfront** is attractive and long; at its end is a decent beach, **Playa Brazomar**. At the other end of the harbour a couple of imposing buildings stand high over the town. The **castle**, now a lighthouse and space used for temporary exhibitions, preserves its Templar walls; nearby, the massive **church** is a surprising building of great architectural and artistic merit. The reliefs on the outside present strange but damaged allegorical scenes of animals kissing and other exotica, while the interior is beautifully Gothic, all arches and blue stained glass; the holy water is kept in a giant clam shell. A picturesque medieval bridge stands nearby. Further around the headland is a beautiful sheltered **rockpool**, occasionally used as a venue for concerts. Also worth checking is the extravagant and eclectic architecture of the early 20th-century **Toki-Eder** mansion on the main road leading east out of the centre.

Castro Urdiales is big on *traineras*, large rowing boats that are raced in regattas on the sea in fierce competition with other towns. These are testosterone-fuelled events that draw big crowds.

West of Castro, the village of **Islares** has a decent beach, but even better is **Oriñ** , excellent stretch of sand dramatically set between rocky mountains, not too spoiled by t somewhat tasteless development behind it.

Santander and around listings

For sleeping and eating price codes and other relevant information, see pages 13-19.

🛌 Where to stay

Santander *p26, map p28*
As befits its resort status, Santander has dozens of places to stay. Many of these are in lofty price brackets, especially in the beachside barrio of Sardinero. There are several cheap *pensiones* around the bus and train stations, most fairly respectable if a bit noisy. Prices in Jul-Aug are outrageously high. Rates drop significantly once the summer rush is over.

€€€€ Hotel Bahía, C Alfonso XIII 6, T942 205 000, www.gruposardinero.com. Standing proud overlooking the port and the bay, this modern hotel delivers not just on location but also on service, facilities and food. Rooms are spacious, with big beds to stretch out on, and great views over the water. You can get good deals via the website or packages with **Brittany Ferries**. Recommended.

€€€€ Hotel Vincci Puertochico, 🖊 C Castelar 25, T942 225 200, www.vincci hoteles.com. With a great location right on the marina, this is a 4-star hotel with compact but comfortable rooms, the best of which look over the water. These cost about €25 more but are worth the extra. Overall, summer prices are too high for this standard of accommodation but you might feel the situation is worth it or get a better deal via a website. Can drop to **€€** off season.

€€€€ Husa Hotel Real, Paseo de Pérez Galdós 28, T942 272 550, www.hotelreal.es. Santander's top hotel was commissioned by the king when the royal family started summering here in the early 20th century.

It's a luxurious and magnificent palace with a French feel to the decor; it has superb views over the bay and prices to match (a double in summer can cost up to €380). It's a byword for style and sophistication in these parts and has seen its fair share of celebrity guests.

€€€ Hotel Chiqui, Av García Lago 9, T902 282 700, www.hotelchiqui.com. This large hotel is well placed at the quiet end of the Sardinero beaches. While service and staff aren't as professional as the **Real**, the front rooms have all the conveniences and superb views out to sea. Excellent off-season and weekend specials are on offer on the website.

€€ Hostal Carlos III, Av Reina Victoria 135, T942 271 616, www.hostalcarlos3.com. Quality beachfront accommodation doesn't always cost the earth. This century-old building offers light, comfortable rooms that offer pretty good value for Santander. Best, however, are the delightful owners.

€€ Jardín Secreto, C Cisneros 37, T942 070 714, www.jardinsecretosantander. com. This unusual, romantic place offers the substantial comfort and attentive welcome of a boutique hotel at the prices of a much inferior establishment. The rooms are individually decorated and delightful and there is indeed, a pretty little garden to relax in. Recommended.

€€ La Corza, C Hernán Cortés 25, T942 212 950. The only accommodation option in the heart of tapas and restaurant territory, this family-run spot sits right on the central Plaza del Pombo, a 1-min walk from the water. There's an old-fashioned austerity about the place, but the rooms are spotlessly clean and spacious, and come with or without bathroom.

Porticada, C Méndez Núñez 17, www.hlaporticada.com. ...r the ferry and bus station, friendly budget option. Most of the rooms have a mirador, and come with or without bathroom. The price difference is small, but there's nothing wrong with the spotless shared washrooms.

€ Pensión Real, Plaza de la Esperanza 1, T942 225 787, pensionreal@hotmail.com. Good-value rooms in a warm and well-maintained family home. A very good deal at this price and located a block behind the town hall.

Camping

Camping Cabo Mayor, Ctra del Faro s/n, T942 391 542, www.cabomayor.com, is a year-round campsite on the Cabo Mayor headland, near the lighthouse and Mataleñas beach north of Sardinero. The appealing location is complemented by great facilities including a pool and bungalows sleeping 2 or 4. It gets packed in summer so book ahead. Bus No 15 will take you there from the centre of town.

South of Santander *p31*

€€€ Gran Hotel Balneario, C Manuel Pérez Mazo s/n, Puente Viesgo, T942 598 061, www.balneariodepuenteviesgo.com. The waters of the town are reportedly effective for skin disorders and rheumatism; this massive spa hotel complex is the place to take them. These types of places are popular in Spain, and there are all manner of treatments available, as well as fine food, well-appointed rooms and pleasant grounds.

Liérganes *p31*

€€ Casona El Arral, C El Convento, T942 528 475, www.casonaelarral.com. The imposing bulk of this mansion sits on the edge of the old town, complete with its own baroque chapel. Rooms though, have a lighter touch, with plenty of space, and a warm, country-house feel. There are spacious grassy grounds and enough

modern comforts like Wi-Fi to make for a very pleasant stay. Breakfast but no other meals available.

Santoña and Escalante *p32*

€€€ San Román de Escalante, Ctra Escalante–Castillo s/n, T942 677 728, www.sanromandeescalante.com. This luxurious complex offers quality accommodation and excellent dining in a complex of modern and historic buildings near Escalante village. From the main road, turn into the village, then head through it and out the other side towards Castillo. 2 km further, you'll find the place, across the road from a gorgeous little Romanesque chapel.

€€ Posada Rivera de Escalante, C La Rivera 1, Escalante, T942 677 719, www.posadalarivera.com. On the main road through Escalante, this is a delightful *casa rural* decorated with a personal touch and much elan and colour. The rooms are invitingly rustic, with exposed beams and varnished floorboards, and there's warm personal service, Wi-Fi, advice on what to see in the surrounding area, and a truly great breakfast (€5-6 extra). Recommended.

Laredo *p32*

Most places to stay are unattractive but functional beach hotels, though surprisingly few are right on the beachfront road. There are also numerous apartments for rental.

€€ Miramar, Alto de Laredo s/n, T942 610 367, www.hmiramarlaredo.com. It would be staggering if there hadn't been a hotel of this name in Laredo; this isn't close to the sand but it has the best views in town, magnificent perspectives over the beach and bay from the steep road leading up to the Bilbao motorway. Apart from that it's simple but comfortable, and lonely but well-priced off-season.

€€ Pensión Esmeralda, Fuente Fresnedo 6, T942 605 219. Set in the old, hilly part of town this has attractive, clean doubles with bath. It's a good budget option and has a café downstairs that'll sort you out with breakfast for €2 extra.

€ Albergue Casa de la Trinidad, C San Francisco 24, T942 606 141. One of 2 hostels in the old town run by nuns, this sparklingly clean place is to be found up the side of the church of the same name; head through a metal gate. Facilities are excellent, with a good kitchen and comfy dorms, and the nuns (who are cloistered; if you need anything you speak to them through a hatch). When speaking to nuns, the convention is to address them *Ave María Purísima*, to which the stock reply is *Sin pecado concebida* (Hail Mary most pure/ Conceived without sin).

€ Pensión Salomón, C Menéndez Pelayo 11, T942 605 081, is an excellent option despite an unremarkable exterior.

Castro Urdiales and around *p32*

€€€ Hotel Las Rocas, C Flaviobriga 1, T942 860 400, www.lasrocashotel.com. Dominating the town beach, this large hotel has spacious rooms, most with sea view, and attentive service. It's pretty good value for its location and standard.

€€ Pensión La Mar, C La Mar 1, Castro Urdiales, T942 870 524. A simpler choice than **La Sota**, this central *pensión* is a good bet with decent en suite rooms with TV and heating. Some rooms have a streetside balcony; there's free Wi-Fi on offer too.

€€ Pensión La Sota, C Correría 1, Castro Urdiales, T942 871 188. This good-looking and sparklingly clean place is wonderfully located a street back from the water. The rooms come with TV and bathroom and are slightly overpriced in summer but good value at other times.

Camping

There's a campsite at **Oriñón** and a summer-only *fonda*; **Islares** is only a 20-min walk and has more to offer.

🍴 Restaurants

Santander *p26, map p28*

Santander's status as elegant holiday resort and active fishing port means there are a good selection of excellent places to eat. Top seafood restaurants and smart wine and *pincho* bars compete for attention with characterful ex-wine cellars and no-frills joints serving the best of fresh fish. Sardinero has excellent eating options, but for concentration and character, head for the old town: the streets backing the Paseo de Pereda, and especially around **Plaza Cañadío**, which is packed on summer nights. If you're travelling on a budget, ask the price before selecting a gourmet bar-top snack.

€€€ Bar del Puerto, C Peña Herbosa 22, T942 212 939, www.bardelpuerto.com. One of the more upmarket choices on this foody stretch, this sleek spot serves up excellent tapas downstairs and seafood upstairs. After hours the lights dim and it becomes a cool and stylish bar.

€€€ La Posada del Mar, C Castelar 19, T942 213 023, www.laposadadelmar.es. Closed Sun and all Sep. A well-established restaurant with a formidable wine list that's moved to newer premises just around the corner from its old haunts. They trot down to the local *lonja* daily for fish – try a whole salt-baked one, they're memorably juicy – but also demonstrate their know-how with meat and game bird dishes.

€€ Balneario la Magdalena, C La Horadada s/n, T942 032 107, www.balneario lamagdalena.com. Excellently located café and restaurant on the peaceful and calm Magdalena beach. The dining room inevitably has fantastic views and the seafood is of the highest order without breaking the bank. There's a huge range of fish and other dishes; the red mullet (*salmonete*) with a sea-urchin sauce is particularly good.

€€ Bodega Cigaleña, C Daoíz y Velarde 19. This warm, snug narrow bar is lined with wooden cabinets. It looks like the workshop of a mad alchemist convinced that the philosopher's stone was to be found at the bottom of a bottle of Rioja or *anis*. An excellent place for tapas, but you can also sit down for a meal; the menu focuses on game and other hearty fare. Recommended.

€€ Bodegas Bringas, C Hernán Cortés 47, T942 362 070. Closed Tue. An excellent tapas bar, one of several set in old wine merchants' warehouses. The atmosphere is great and the food good and well priced. It's a convivial spot with a tasty array of *pinchos* adorning its long bar.

€€ Bodega del Riojano, C Río de la Pila 5, T942 216 750. This loveable bodega has what is, for Spain, an almost reverentially hushed atmosphere as people seem awed by the ageing wine bottles that line the place from floor to ceiling. This old wine merchants' is famous for its decoratively painted barrels. The *tortilla con bonito* (tuna omelette) is the best around, while there's a range of cheeses, cured meats and stews. *Raciones* cost €6-12. Closed for extensive renovations at last visit.

€€ Casa Albo, C Peña Herbosa 15, T942 213 057, www.casaalbo.iespana.es. This unassuming place is long-standing, family-run and produces some of Northern Spain's best paella, made with locally caught seafood. It really is sensational. Recommended.

€€ Casa Lita, Paseo Pereda 37, T942 364 830, www.casalita.es. Sporting a range of well-presented bar-top *pinchos* that won't break the bank, this features snug seating along the stone-clad wall and helpful service. Just browse the selection and pick something that takes your fancy – from basics such as delicious tortilla, to posher fare like duck ham canapés.

€ Bodegas Manzón, C Hernán Cortés 57, T942 215 752. Open daily. This cavernous bar is big enough to park several buses in and is a Santander institution, having been in business more than a century. The huge

vats of wine have the menu of cheap and cheerful *raciones* chalked up on the side; the smaller barrels still bear the names of the sherries and other wines that were once shipped from the port here. Chunky wooden tables and down-to-earth staff and customers add to the atmosphere. *Raciones* €3-10.

€ La Conveniente, C Gómez Oreña 9, T942 212 887. Open Mon-Sat from 1900. Another atmospheric bodega by Plaza Cañadío with a spacious, beamed interior, several shiploads of wine and a good variety of cheap food. It's a memorable place with its art nouveau panels about the only adornment to the chipped marble and aged wood, all with a patina of decades of chatter accompanied by a pianist on a honky-tonk keyboard.

€ La Gaviota, C Marqués de la Ensenada 35, T942 221 106. One of a series of downmarket but deservedly popular seafood restaurants in a block of the Barrio Pesquero, an earthy zone by the fishing harbour. All of them offer cheap, cheerful, and generously proportioned *raciones* of fish and seafood, as well as paella. Sardines or anything else off the grill are recommendable.

Other spots in the Barrio Pesquero include the small but excellent **La Chulilla**, and the popular **Los Peñucos**, run by the father of football star Iván de la Peña. Take bus No 4 or 14 from anywhere on the Santander waterfront to get here.

€ Las Hijas de Florencio, Paseo de Pereda 23, T686 160 260. Old-time in feel, with its ancient floor of coloured tiles and high ceiling, this amicable double-entrance bar draws an animated local crowd from morning coffee time onwards. Tasty and fairly priced bartop snacks, an optimistic buzz, a takeaway cheese counter, and plenty of wine make this a favourite.

Cafés
Café Suizo, Paseo de Pereda 28, T942 215 864. This large and light 2-level café's white

wooden balustrades give it the feeling of a film set. It's well known as one of the best breakfast spots in town, with a range of sandwiches, pastries and little rolls, as well as a large terrace out on the waterfront road.
La Casa del Indiano, Mercado del Este s/n, T942 074 660. The recently renovated 19th-century market now houses a variety of specialist shops (including a good little wine shop), as well as this cheerful café/bar that takes up half the building and makes a great stop at any time of day.

Santoña and Escalante *p32*
€€€ San Román de Escalante, Escalante s/n, T942 677 728, www.sanromande escalante.com. Some 2 km from the village of Escalante, this restaurant is set superbly in an old mansion house furnished with beautiful art and antiques. The cuisine is of the highest order; the memorable seafood, such as monkfish on crab paste, has won it many plaudits. Rooms also available (see Where to stay).

Laredo *p32*
For tapas, restaurants and bars, head up the steps next to the town hall to the cobbled old-town street **C Rúamayor**, a long, narrow affair with plentiful choice.
€€ La Abadía, C Rúamayor 18, T942 611 489, www.mesonlaabadia.com. Attractively set in a house partly dating from the 15th century, this restaurant has a fairly traditional sort of Spanish menu drawing from different parts of the country. The paella is excellent, as is the roast lamb, but don't decide until you've found out what the stew of the day is (*guiso del día*).

Castro Urdiales and around *p32*
Castro has a good eating scene, with plenty of fish restaurants and, along C Rúa, running parallel to the waterside, a series of simple but convivial tapas bars: try **La Bodeguita** at C Ardigales 4 also has some good eating options.

€€ El Puerto, C Santa María s/n, T942 870 976, www.asadorelpuerto.com. Perched on top of the *lonja* by the fishing harbour, just below the church, this spot has a fabulous covered terrace offering great views over the bobbing boats and charming waterside. The menu looks seaward, with juicy mussels, tuna *ventresca* (tender meat from the belly region), and anchovies all tasty.
€€ El Segoviano, Plaza del Ayuntamiento s/n, T942 861 859. On the main plaza a few steps from the waterfront, this low-beamed restaurant serves up heavier fare than the seafood-based places that characterize Castro. Roast meats are the order of the day, with suckling pig a particularly tender speciality.
€€ Mesón Marinero, Plaza del Ayuntamiento s/n, T942 860 005, www.mesonmarinero.com. An excellent restaurant with a wooden terrace, under the arcade in the main plaza. The seafood, of which there is a huge variety, is superb and is allowed to stand on its own merits rather than being smothered in other flavours. The *marmitakos* (spicy Basque fish stews) are especially tasty, and the grilled sardines reliably good.

🕪 Bars and clubs

Santander *p26, map p28*
Blues, C Gómez Oreña 15, T942 314 305. A packed and popular bar with a good mix of people. The music, as you may have guessed, rests on a base of blues and soul.
Floridita, C Bailén s/n. A cheerful and very lively bar, with a youngish crowd and unpretentious scene. It's got a Cuban theme, a little terrace, free Wi-Fi, and a fine attitude. They specialize in daiquiris and mojitos.
Rocambole, C Hernán Cortés 24. A late-running bar with frequent live jazz and blues and a fun dancefloor. There are often 'open jam' nights where anyone with an instrument can join in.

Ventilador, Plaza Cañadío s/n. A popular bar with outdoor tables on this lively night-time square. The atmosphere is a bit more relaxing in the quieter early evening; later on in summer it's more or less a take-away for people congregating in the square.

Laredo *p32*

Cafe IV, C Rúa Mayor 12. More a bar than a café, this cheerful nightspot is decorated with pseudo-Egyptian murals and has a few tables out on the street that are eagerly sought after. As well as a selection of wines, they have a couple of Belgian beers on tap.

🔅 Entertainment

Santander *p26, map p28*
Bahía Cinema, Av Marqués de la Hermida s/n, www.cinesa.es. A big-release cinema.
Filmoteca de Cantabria, C Bonifaz 6, T942 319 310. Arthouse films and movie festivals.
Gran Casino, Plaza Italia s/n. Open 2000-0400 (0500 in summer). Dress code and proof of age regulations apply. There's a €5 cover charge.
Palacio de Festivales, C Castelar s/n. A spacious venue for concerts and exhibitions.

🎊 Festivals

Santander *p26, map p28*
28 Jul The province's main rowing regatta takes place during Semana Grande, Santander's major fiesta.
Aug International Festival, www.festival santander.com. Santander's major event of the year, with some top musical and theatrical performances. The liveliest street action comes at its end, which coincides with the fiesta of the city's patron saints.

🛍 Shopping

Santander *p26, map p28*
Santander's main shopping streets are near the town hall, cathedral and to the west.

Librería Estudio, Paseo Calvo Sotelo 19. A good bookshop with a largish selection.

⏱ What to do

Santander *p26, map p28*
Racing Santander, www.realracingclub.es, yo-yo between the *Primera* and *Segunda* divisions in Spanish football. At time of writing, they had been in the top flight for a little while, and entertain the likes of **Real Madrid** in their stadium in Sardinero. Tickets can be bought at the stadium on Fri and Sat for a Sun fixture, as well as from 2 hrs before the game.

⊖ Transport

Santander *p26, map p28*
Air
Air services arrive at the Parayas airport, 5 km southwest of the centre. **ALSA** runs buses to the airport every 30 mins or so (€1.50, 15 mins), and also connect the airport directly with other cities, such as **Laredo** and **Bilbao**, check their website www.alsa.es for timetables. A taxi costs about €15 from the centre. **Ryanair** currently serve this airport from **London** Stansted, **Rome** Ciampino, **Dublin**, **Frankfurt** Hahn, Weeze, and **Milan** Orio al Serio, as well as from **Madrid**, **Alicante** and **Reus**. Iberia run domestic flights from here to **Barcelona** and **Madrid** as well as other Spanish cities. The airport phone number is T942 251 004.
    Airlines Iberia, Plaza Pombo s/n, www.iberia.es.

Bus
There's a handy online timetable at www. santandereabus.com, or you can phone the bus station on T942 211 995. Many buses ply routes from Santander to other Spanish cities. 5 a day go to **Burgos** (3 hrs) and on to **Madrid** (6 hrs, €29), while buses east to **Bilbao** (90 mins, €7) are almost hourly. Several a day follow the coast westwards as far as **Gijón** and **Oviedo**

(10 daily, 2½-3 hrs), while there are also buses serving **Zaragoza**, **Valladolid**, **A Coruña** and others.

Within Cantabria, there are 5 daily buses (2 on Sun) running to **Santillana del Mar** (40 mins) and **Comillas** (55 mins) and 10-15 daily buses to **San Vicente de la Barquera** (1 hr if direct). **Laredo** is served roughly hourly, as is **Castro Urdiales** (1¼ hrs), while for the **Picos de Europa**, there are 1-3 buses daily to **Potes**, some of which have a connection to **Fuente Dé**.

Car
Car hire Atesa, C Marcelino Sanz de Santuola, T942 222 926, www.atesa.es; Hertz, Puerto Ferrys, T942 362 821, www.hertz.es.

Ferry
Brittany Ferries, T0871 244 0744, www.brittany-ferries.co.uk, run a service from **Plymouth** and **Portsmouth**, UK, to Santander. There's 1 weekly sailing on each route, taking around 24 hrs from Portsmouth and 20 hrs from Plymouth. Prices are variable but can usually be found for about €80-100 each way in a reclining seat. A car adds about €170 each way, and cabins start from about €90. The service runs from mid-Mar to mid-Nov.

Taxi
If none on the street call, T942 333 333.

Train
Santander is both on the national **RENFE** network and the private coastal **FEVE** service.

The stations are next to each othe bus station). Call the RENFE static 280 202; the FEVE station on T94

RENFE runs 3 trains daily to **Madrid** (4½-5 hrs, €48) and 7 or so to **Valladolid** and **Palencia** on the same line. There are *cercanía* trains to **Torrelavega** and **Reinosa** every 30 mins.

FEVE trains run east to **Bilbao** 3 times daily (2½ hrs, €9) and west along the coast as far as **Oviedo**, **Gijón** and **Ferrol** in Galicia twice daily (to Oviedo/Gijón, it's 4 hrs and costs €16). It's a fairly slow but scenic service, and invaluable for accessing smaller coastal towns.

South of Santander *p31*
Bus
Puente Viesgo is accessible by bus from **Santander** (operated by various companies; 40 mins) up to 6 times daily. **Liérganes** is served 4 times daily (40 mins). Liérganes is also served by regular FEVE *cercanía* train from Santander.

Laredo *p32*
Bus
Frequent buses connected Laredo and **Santander** (every 30 mins, 40 mins).

Castro Urdiales and around *p32*
Bus
Castro Urdiales is connected very regularly by bus with both **Santander** (more than hourly, 80 mins) and **Bilbao**, which is only 30 mins away.

West Coast of Cantabria

Cantabria's western coast has plenty to detain the visitor. As well as some good beaches, there are some very attractive towns; these are headed up by Santillana del Mar, a superb ensemble of stonework that also boasts the flash museum at nearby Altamira, the site of some of the finest prehistoric art ever discovered. Comillas will appeal to fans of modernista architecture and, beyond, the coast continues towards Asturias, backed spectacularly by the bulky Picos de Europa mountains. There are some fine beaches right along this stretch.

Santillana del Mar and around → *For listings, see pages 43-46.*

Although it may sound like a seaside town, it isn't; it's 4 km inland. A cynical old saying claims that it's the town of three lies: '*Santillana no es santa, no es llana, y no hay mar*' (Santillana's neither holy nor flat, and there's no sea). Nevertheless, Santillana is delightful, despite the high number of strolling visitors captivated by the architecture of the place that Sartre immortalized (albeit in *Nausea*) as "the most beautiful village in Spain". While it's still a dairy region – cows are still brought back into the village in the evening – every building within the old town is now devoted to tourism in some form. It's definitely worth staying overnight, as the bulk of the visitors are on day trips, and the emptier the town, the more atmospheric it is. Try and come out of season, and avoid weekends if possible. The nearby Altamira museum is also a big draw for visitors.

Background
Founded by monks, the town became important in the Middle Ages due to the power of its monastery, which had a finger in every pie cooking. What the town is today is a result of the nobility wresting control of the feudal rent system from the abbot in the 15th century. Once the peasants were filling secular coffers, the landowners grew wealthy, donated money in exchange for titles and started trying to outdo each other in ostentatious *palacio* construction. Though undoubtedly antidemocratic and tasteless at the time, these buildings are exceedingly beautiful.

Places in Santillana del Mar
The **tourist office** ① *C Jesús Otero 20, T942 818 251, santillana@cantabria.org, daily 0900-1330, 1600-1900*, at the edge of the old town near the main road, is busy and brusque. They supply a decent map/guide to the town in a variety of languages.

The **Colegiata** ① *daily 1000-1330, 1600-1830 (closes 1930 in summer), €3 (includes entrance to the Diocesan Museum at the other end of town)*, sits at the end of the town and has a jumbled, homely façade in orangey stone. The current Romanesque building replaced a former Benedictine monastery in the 12th century. An arcaded gallery runs high above the portal, and a round belltower to the right outrages symmetry fans. Wander around the side to gain access to the church and cloister, whose shady Romanesque arches also feature many different motifs on the capitals, ranging from mythological creatures to geometric figures and Biblical scenes.

The church is spacious with impressive stone vaulting; there is some of the *ajedrezado jaqués* chessboard patterning originally used in the town of Jaca and disseminated through Northern Spain by wandering masons and pilgrims. The building is dedicated to Santa Juliana, a third-century saint for whom the town is named. She was put to death by her husband for not consummating their marriage on their wedding night (or any other night); her bones were originally brought here by the community of monks that founded the monastery and town. One of her achievements in life was the taming of a demon, whom she used to drag around on a rope (to the despair of their marriage counsellor); scenes from her life can be seen on her tomb in the centre of the church, and the *retablo*, a 16th-century work. There's a figure of Juliana in the centre, standing above a chest that holds various parts of her earthly remains.

The other major sight in town is the collection of grandiose *palacios* emblazoned with coats-of-arms (in some cases hugely oversized). They are concentrated down the main street, **Calle Cantón**, and around the main square. The square has two Gothic towers, one of which is an exhibition hall. In front of the church, the former **abbot's house** was later occupied by the Archduchess of Austria; further down this street note the former marquis' house (now a hotel). The **Casa de los Villa** near the main road has a façade emblazoned with a pierced eagle and the motto *un buen morir es honra de la vida* (a good death honours the life); a precursor to the Falangist Civil War cry ¡*Viva la muerte!*

As Santillana is a popular place to spend holidays, there's always plenty on for young and old, with frequent temporary exhibitions, craft displays and festivals. Permanent attractions include a decent **zoo** ⓘ *www.zoosantillanadelmar.com, daily 0930-dusk, €16, kids €10*, on the edge of town, which has a snow leopard among its constricted but cared-for captives. There is a **Torture Museum** ⓘ *daily 1000-2000, 2200 in summer, €4*, near the church with all sorts of horrible fantasies in iron used during the Inquisition and other dark periods in human history. Near the church, the **Fundación Jesús Otero** ⓘ *Plaza Francisco Navarro s/n, T942 840 198, daily 1000-1330, 1600-1930 (1700-2100 summer), free*, displays works by the 20th-century sculptor of the same name, a Santillana local. The **Diocesan Museum** ⓘ *Tue-Sun 1000-1330, 1600-1830 (closes 1930 summer, also open Mon); joint ticket with the Colegiata, €3*, on the main road, which is a good example of its kind, has a large collection that includes some Latin American pieces brought back to Santillana by *indianos*.

Altamira Caves

ⓘ *T942 818 005, http://museodealtamira.mcu.es, Jun-Sep Tue-Sat 0930-1930, Sun 0930-1500, Oct-May Tue-Sat 0930-1700, Sun 0930-1500, last admission to the Neocueva 1 hr before closing; €3, free Sat after 1430 and Sun all day. To apply to visit the original cave, write to the museum at Museo de Altamira, 39330 Santillana del Mar, or at informacion.maltamira@mcu. es, but you have to have a serious scientific reason to gain admission.*

In 1879, in the countryside 2 km from Santillana, a man and his daughter were exploring some caves only discovered a few years before when they looked up and saw a cavalcade of animals superbly painted in ochre and charcoal. The man, Marcelino Sanz de Sautuola, was interested in prehistoric art, but the quality of these works far exceeded any known at the time. Excitedly publishing his findings, he wasn't believed until several years after his death, when the discovery of similar paintings in southern France made the sceptics reverse their position. The paintings are amazing; fluid bison, deer and horses, some 14,000 years old. They became a major tourist attraction, but the moist breath of the visitors began to damage the art and admission had to be restricted; the waiting list is about three years at present and may be entirely terminated in the future. Enter the Neocueva. It's a replica of part of the original cave and paintings and is part of a museum that puts the art in context. The exhibition begins with an excellent overview of prehistoric hominids so you can get your Neanderthals sorted from your Cro-Magnons before moving on to more specific displays about the Altamira epoch and ways of life at the time.

The Neocueva itself is accessed in groups with a guide; there can be quite a wait if the museum is busy. It's an impressive reconstruction, and the explanations are good. You can admire the replica paintings, particularly as they were probably painted from a prone position but, although impressive, they lack some of the emotion that comes from actually feeling the incomprehensible gulf of 14,000 years. All told, it's a very good museum and an impressive substitute for the original cave, which the government were absolutely right to protect from destruction.

Suances

This low-key summer resort northeast of Santillana has a series of fine sandy beaches popular with swimmers and surfers alike. Playa de los Locos, with a picturesque setting backed by cliffs, is one of the best for riding the waves, but it gets busy. La Tablia, the next one along, has consistent surf too. Don't leave valuables in your car in the clifftop parking at these places.

Comillas

Comillas is a fashionable Cantabrian beach resort and has been popular with the well-to-do for over a century. As well as its beach and pleasant old centre, the town is worth a visit for its architecture, out of the ordinary for a seaside summer town. Rather than drab lines of holiday cottages, it boasts some striking modernista buildings ostentatiously perched on the hilltops around the town. They are a legacy of Catalan architects who were commissioned by competitive local aristocrats to create suitably extravagant residences for them. The **tourist office** ① *T942 722 591, oficinadeturismo@comillas.es, daily 0930-1330, 1600-1900 (1700-2000 summer)*, in the town hall building on the main road through Comillas, is efficient and helpful.

The town's most unusual architectural flourishes are found in Gaudí's *El Capricho*. Rightly named (the caprice), it's an astonishingly imaginative flight of fancy embossed with bright green and yellow tiles and adorned with Mediterranean sunflowers. The best feature is a whimsical tower, an ornate Muslim fantasy with a balcony. The restaurant that occupied the interior is now closed, so the only access is via the Palacio de Sobrellano.

Next door to El Capricho is the **Palacio de Sobrellano** ① *Apr-Jun and Sep-Oct Tue-Sun 0930-1400, Jul and Aug daily 1000-2100, €3 palace, €3 chapel (guided tour)*, commissioned by the Marqués de Comillas, a heavy pseudo-Gothic structure full of quirky furniture. A small plot in the parish graveyard wasn't the marquis's vision of resting in peace, so he had an ornate chapel put up next to the family summer home to hold flashy tombs that would have done justice to a Renaissance monarch.

On the eminence opposite, the **Universidad Pontificia** was built as a theological college in similarly avant-garde style. It's a majestic and grandiose structure in reddish stone that dominates the town. Whether the priests-in-training were imbued with Christian humility in such a building is open to question, but in any event the college moved to Madrid in 1964. The building is now subject to various plans for its future and is not open for visits.

The town itself has several attractive squares and mansions that seem positively modest by comparison. Keep your eyes up as you wander around to appreciate some of the fine carved balustrades. The cobbled Plaza de la Constitución is at the heart of the area and is winningly beautiful, with fabulous balconies and rustic rubble masonry. There are two good beaches 10 minutes' walk from the centre. West of Comillas is another strand, **Playa Oyambre**, with a campsite and cheap but tasty restaurant.

San Vicente de la Barquera

Although blessed with a stunning mountain backdrop (when you can see it for the mist), San Vicente is a fairly low-key although pleasant resort. While the town's seafood restaurants and natural setting at the mouth of two rivers appeal, the attractive old-town streets have been surrounded by some fairly thoughtless modern development. The architectural highlight is the transitional Gothic **Iglesia de Nuestra Señora de los Angeles**, which has a wooden floor like a ship's deck and attractive Gothic vaulting. The church was built in the 13th century, when Romanesque was going pointy, and it's an interesting example of this phase. There are good views from here over the river estuary and the long bridge crossing it.

On the same ridge, the **castle** ① *Tue-Sun 1030-1330, 1600-1800 (1700-2000 summer), €1.20*, is in reasonable shape but isn't overly compelling. There's an exhibition of the town's history inside. The big **tourist office** ① *Av Generalísimo 20, T942 710 797, daily 0930-1330, 1600-1900, turismosanvicente@cantabria.org*, is on the main street; the Fascist street names live on for some reason.

West Coast of Cantabria listings

For sleeping and eating price codes and other relevant information, see pages 13-19.

● Where to stay

Santillana del Mar *p40*
Santillana has a great selection of characterful old-town hotels, but it also has several that are less appealingly situated on the main road, or worse, in an ugly expansion on the other side of it that tried to retain that old-town look but failed. However, there are enough in the old centre itself to make sure you end up there, though you should definitely book ahead in summer. Many private homes put signs out advertising *camas* or *habitaciones* at peak time; some of these are very good options.

€€€€ La Casa del Marqués, C Cantón 26, T942 818 888, www.turismosantillana delmar.com. Santillana's priciest hotel is excellently set in a large *palacio* that belonged to the local marquis, who had to display his superior status with 3 coats of arms. The interior decoration is simpler, with attractive wooden furniture but numerous facilities. Service lets down the overall effect, but it's still a memorable place to stay.

€€€€ Parador Gil Blas, Plaza Ramón Pelayo 11, T942 028 028, www.parador.es. In a modernized *palacio* on the beautifully bare Plaza Mayor, this parador is named after a famous fictional character from Santillana created by the French novelist Lesage in the 18th century. There's a good restaurant, and the rooms have every comfort. Another parador, **Parador Santillana**, sits on the same square, and is slightly cheaper, but not much more so, and it's not quite as appealing.

€€€ Altamira, C Cantón 1, T942 818 025, www.hotelaltamira.com. This is cheaper than the preceding options but also characterfully set in another sumptuous *palacio*, with appropriate decor. The patio restaurant is a picturesque spot for a drink, but the food is overpriced for what it is.

€€ Esmeralda, C Antonio López 7,
T942 720 097, www.hostalesmeralda.com.
This good, friendly choice is right in the
centre, set in a great old stone building.
The rooms are large (with good duplex
family units) and sensitively modernized,
good off-season prices on offer (**€€-€**).
Restaurant downstairs.

€€ Hotel Joseín, C Manuel Noriega 27,
T942 720 225, www.hoteljosein.com. On
the eastern side of town, this rather ugly
budget hotel doesn't look up to much
from outside, but its position more than
makes up for it. Perched right over the
beach, it boasts stunning sea views from
the big windows of all the rooms. An extra
€20 gets you a balcony hanging over the
sand. There's an on-site restaurant with
overpriced seafood but a €12 menú del día.

€€ Pensión Vega de Pas, Paseo del
Muelle 9, T942 722 102. An upmarket
pensión with good facilities, this is comfy
if not stylish and overlooks the beach
5-10 mins' walk from the centre of town.

€€ Posada Ansorena y Echevarria,
C Cantón 10, T942 818 228, ansorena@
hotmail.com. This delightful stone mansion
is right on the main cobbled street and
makes a great place to stay. Inside it's all
rustic dark wooden furniture and creaking
floorboards; rooms are large and varied,
many with a balcony overlooking the
garden. There's also a guest lounge with
board games. Breakfast included; very
good value.

€€ Posada La Casa del Organista, C Los
Hornos 4, T942 840 352, www.casadel
organista.com. Set in a smaller but still
impressive 18th-century home; this is a
welcoming place with lovely wooden
furnishings and rustic bedrooms. The
quality of the welcome, the stone walls,
old-time atmosphere, and sharp off-season
prices (**€€**) make this a great place.
Recommended.

€€ Posada las Ijanas, Barrio la Puentuca
10, Vivedo, T942 888 964, www.posadalas
ijanas.com. 3 km east of Santillana on the
CA-131, this is an appealing rural hotel
decorated in rustic style. There are few
rooms, all new and thoughtfully appointed.
The owners are very friendly and can advise
on walking in the area. Breakfast features
home-baking and fresh juices and can be
taken on the patio.

€ Casa Octavio, Plaza de las Arenas s/n,
T942 818 199, www.hospedajeoctavio.com.
A peaceful and very attractive spot to find
a bed in an alley off the Plaza de las Arenas
by the side of the church. There's a variety
of rooms on offer.

San Vicente de la Barquera p43

You'll have no problems finding a room on
spec; there are many places.

€€ Hotel Luzón, Av Miramar 1, T942 710
050, www.hotelluzon.net. This imposing
centenarian mansion dominates the heart
of town, and its attractive recent conversion
to a hotel makes it San Vicente's most
recommendable accommodation choice.
It's not as luxurious as you might imagine
from the outside but it's comfortable;
spacious rooms, some with water views,
eager-to-please staff, fair prices, and modern
conveniences make it a sound choice.

€ Pensión Liébana, C Ronda 2, T942
710 211. This pensión is right in the
centre of things and has decent rooms
with bathroom and TV, which become
exceedingly cheap once summer is over.

🍴 Restaurants

Santillana del Mar p40

The hotel restaurants are rather
unremarkable, and disappointingly there's
no eating option that reaches the same
standard as some of the sleeping choices.
There are several tourist-trap places too.

€€ El Castillo, Plaza Mayor 6, T942
818 377, www.elcastillosantillana.com.
Although in the heart of the town, this
bar/restaurant next to the parador is
refreshingly unpretentious and does
some good dishes at reasonable prices.

The *menú de cocido* is particularly hearty; broth followed by a big serve of chickpeas and stewed pork cuts. There's a *menú del día* for €14.

€€ Gran Duque, C Escultor Jesús Otero Orena, www.granduque.com. Closed Jan-Feb. The most appealing of the town's restaurants, this has views over the surrounding meadows and a warmly welcoming interior with brick, wooden beams, and clay tiles. There's much attractive seafood on the list, including a delicious seafood salad, and everything's well presented but unpretentious.

Comillas *p42*
Comillas has a reputation for being a pricey place to dine, but the quality is generally good.

€€ Filipinas, C de los Arzobispos s/n, T942 720 375. This is a lively bar on the intersection in the middle of town, where the locals eat. There are simple *raciones* of seafood and meat, as well as hearty stews in tin pots. The abundant €14 *menú del día* is popular, so you'll often wait for a table, especially at weekends.

€€ Gurea, C Ignacio Fernández de Castro 11, T942 722 446. Closed Sun afternoon and Mon. A Basque restaurant that lives up to all the good things that implies. Mains such as *bacalao a la vizcaína* (a cod dish) or *kokotxas* (hake cheeks in spicy sauce; excellent) cost €12-20 and are served in a cosy atmosphere.

€ Siglo, Plaza Constitución 11, T942 722 257. The cosy interior of this family-run bar sports hams, hanging peppers, and just a few tables where you can enjoy solid home-style cooking at decent prices. Ask for whatever's good that day; the *solomillo ibérico*, juicy and tender chunks of prime pork cooked with garlic, is a safely tasty bet.

San Vicente de la Barquera *p43*
There are numerous seafood restaurants along the main street through town, with everything from downmarket bars selling cheap and delicious grilled sardines to upmarket *marisquerías* peddling crustaceans.

€€€ Annua, Paseo de la Barquera s/n, T942 715 050, www.annuagastro.com. With an unforgettable waterside position right on the estuary, this modern restaurant lives up to its location with excellent, creative cuisine. The staple here is seafood: they have their own oyster farm. There's a degustation menu (€66 including drinks) brimming with innovation and light-heartedness. It's a romantic place for a sunset drink too. Recommended.

€€€ Boga-Boga, Av Generalísimo, T942 710 135. The food at Boga-Boga lives up to its excellent name, which is a traditional Basque sea shanty. There's a great variety of seafood – their speciality is a lobster stew for 2 – and some good wines to knock back with it. There are also decent rooms upstairs.

€€ Augusto, C Mercado 1, T942 712 040. This excellent seafood restaurant sees plenty of visitors at its terraced tables and in its ship-like interior. There are plenty of good-value mixed platters to choose from; you can have a good meal here at a number of different price levels depending on what crustaceans take your fancy. They also do a good line in tasty paellas and rices.

🎵 Bars and clubs

Comillas *p42*
Don Porfirio, C Victoriano Pérez de la Riva 2, T942 722 516. In the old town, this is a friendly and boisterous bar with internet access, a Mexican feel, cold beer and pizzas. In summer, the garden gets going, with picnic-style wooden seats on the grass.

Pamara, C Comillas s/n, is a good summer *discoteca* with an upmarket set. There's sometimes live music or other events on winter weekends too.

⊖ Transport

Santillana del Mar *p40*
Bus
There are 5 daily buses (2 on Sun) running
to and from **Santander** (30 mins).

Comillas *p42*
Bus
There are 5 daily buses, 2 on Sun, running
to and from **Santander** via **Santillana
del Mar**. They continue westwards to
San Vicente de Barquera.

San Vicente de la Barquera *p43*
Bus
10-15 daily buses run to **Santander** (1 hr
if direct), some going via **Comillas** and
Santillana. There are also 10 westbound
buses to **Oviedo** and **Gijón**.

Contents

Footprint features

Los Picos de Europa

Los Picos de Europa

The Picos de Europa are a small, compact, mountainous area of the vast Cordillera Cantábrica blessed with spectacular scenery, superb walking, abundant wildlife and, most crucially, comparatively easy access (but take your hat off to the engineers who built the roads). They encompass the corners of three provinces: Asturias, Cantabria and León, and have a relatively mild climate due to their proximity to the sea. It is this proximity to the coast that probably gives them their curious name (the Peaks of Europe); they often would have been the first sight of land that weary Spanish sailors got on their return from the Americas.

The Picos are comprised of three main massifs of limestone cut and tortured over the millennia by glaciation, resulting in the distinctive rock formations typical of the karstic type. The central part of the range is a national park, expanded from the original Parque Nacional de la Montaña de Covadonga, the first such beast in Spain, denominated in 1918.

Arriving in Picos de Europa

Getting there The Picos de Europa are easily accessed from Gijón and Oviedo, or Santander, and are within a couple of hours' drive from León. The two principal towns for Picos tourism are Cangas de Onís (Asturias) and Potes (Cantabria); both make excellent bases, especially if you lack private transport. The main centre of the Leonese Picos is Posada de Valdeón. Potes is serviced regularly by bus from Santander and the Cantabrian coast, while there are frequent buses from Oviedo and Gijón to Cangas. *See Transport, page 58.*

Getting around
Travelling around the Picos de Europa is simple with your own transport and time-consuming without. The Picos is basically a rectangular area with a main road running around its perimeter and several smaller roads dead-ending into the heart of the mountains from it. Buses run on the main roads and to popular destinations like Covadonga and Fuente Dé. Fewer buses run on Sundays; taxis are in any event a reasonable alternative, if there are two or more of you. There are also jeep services that act as shared taxis. Hitching is easy in the Picos too. The ideal way to explore the area is on foot; it's only three hours through the Cares gorge, and you've crossed the Picos from north to south; the journey wouldn't take less by car.

Tourist information
The Picos de Europa National Park offices run free guided tours around the Picos region during summer, an excellent service. The schedule changes each year and is organized from the three regional information centres. All the major towns have year-round tourist offices, and in addition many villages have summer-only kiosks. The best tourist information offices for the Picos are Cangas de Onís and at the Sotamo visitor centre north of Potes. *See Cangas de Onís, page 50, and Potes, page 59.*

Best time to visit
The best time to visit the Picos is either side of high summer; September/October and May/June are ideal, in July and August prices are well up and the crowds can hamper enjoyment of the natural beauties of the area. The Picos have a fairly damp and temperate maritime climate so you're never assured of clear days, but neither does it get extremely cold, at least on the north side of the range. Mists descend regularly; so take a compass and check the forecast. In winter it can snow heavily, particularly in the southern (ie Leonese) part of the range.

Flora and fauna
The Picos are home to a wide variety of fauna and flora, due partly to the hugely varying climactic zones within its terrasculpted interior. Among the birds, vultures are common; rarer are eagles and capercaillies. Less glamorous species include choughs and wallcreepers. Chamois are a reasonably common sight, as are wild boar; there are also mountain cats, wolves and bears about, but they are much scarcer. A frequent and pretty sight on roads are herds of soft-eyed cows of an attractive local species. Insect and reptile life is also abundant; clouds of butterflies are about in spring and summer. The flora varies widely from the temperate to the Alpine; in spring the mountain fields are full of wildflowers.

Asturian Picos

Asturias claims the largest slab of the Picos massif and has the most advanced environmental and tourism infrastructure of the region. The area's main town, Cangas de Onís, is an excellent place to begin a trip to the Picos, while nearby Covadonga is revered as the birthplace of Christian Spain. The area is also famous for the strong blue cheese known as Cabrales after the villages in which it is produced. Similar in style to Roquefort, it lends its flavour to many a gourmet dish, but is also enjoyed by the locals as a smotherer of chips. Some of the most dramatic rocky scenery of the region is accessed south of here; there are some fantastic hikes in the area around Puente Poncebos, including the three-hour gorge walk to Caín, a route that crosses the Picos from north to south.

Cangas de Onís → *For listings, see pages 55-58.*

This service town is a typically cheerful Asturian centre, with plenty of places to stay, and some top *sidrerías* in which to drink and eat. Its highlight is a superb medieval bridge across the Río Sella with an alarmingly steep cobbled arch. It's at its best when eerily floodlit at night; locals inaccurately name it the **Puente Romano** (Roman bridge). Also of interest is the **Ermita de Santa Cruz**, just across the other river (the Güeña), a tiny 15th-century chapel, which has fifth-century origins and was built over a dolmen; the key can be collected from the tourist office.

After his victory at Covadonga (see below), Pelayo set up base here and Cangas proudly claims to be the first capital of Christian Spain as a result. A statue of a very rugged Pelayo stands defiantly outside the church, a 20th-century construction with *indiano* and Italian influences visible in its three-storey belltower. There are many *indiano* buildings in town; a good number of eastern Asturians left to seek their fortunes in the New World.

Cangas' **tourist office** ⓘ *T985 848 005, www.cangasdeonis.com, daily 1000-1400, 1600-1900, Jun-Sep daily 1000-2200*, is the best equipped in the Picos region, with plenty of information about the whole Picos area. Grab all the information you can here, as the smaller offices in other towns have less regular opening and sometimes run out of maps, etc.

Around Cangas

South of Cangas the road to Riaño soon plunges into the Desfiladero de los Beyos. It's a popular spot for walking and salmon fishing and vultures are a common sight.

North of Cangas, the town of **Arriondas** is a popular base for canoeing the Río Sella, but lacks the appeal of Cangas, which also operates canoeing trips. The descent to the coast at Ribadesella is brisk but not too challenging; a fun introduction to the sport. A typical half-day involves transport to the launch point, descent, lunch and return to the town, be it Cangas or Arriondas.

Covadonga → *For listings, see pages 55-58.*

Some 4 km east of Cangas, a side road leads a further 7 km up a wooded valley to Covadonga, a name written large in Spanish history, more for what it represented after the fact than for what it was. Thronged with Spanish pilgrims and visitors, its main touristic interest lies in its pretty setting and in the observation of just how deep the Reconquista is embedded as the country's primary source of national pride.

Background
The facts are few and lost in time and propaganda. What is conjectured is that Pelayo, an Asturian leader, defeated a Moorish expedition here some time around AD 718. Some accounts from the Middle Ages claim that 124,000 Moors were killed here by 30 men. This is an obvious exaggeration, it would seem more likely that the force was of a small expeditionary nature and the defeat a minor one. For the Moors, the defeat was certainly of little military significance; it was another 14 years before their first serious reverse occurred at Poitiers, a good distance into France. But Spanish history has cast Covadonga as the beginning of the Reconquista, the reconquest of the peninsula by Christian soldiers, a process that wasn't complete until 1492, nearly 800 years later. In truth, the battle may have had some effect, at least in establishing Pelayo as pre-eminent among Asturian warlords and sowing the seeds for the foundation of a Christian kingdom in the mountains, a kingdom that eventually did play a significant role in unravelling Muslim dominance in Iberia. But it's hard to sit at Covadonga, watching the coaches roll in, and not ponder on how what in theory is a battleground has become a Christian shrine respected with great devotion.

Sights
The focus of Covadonga is the **cave** where the Christian reconquest of the peninsula allegedly began, a pretty little grotto in a rockface with a waterfall and small chapel. Pelayo is buried here at the scene of his triumph, in a plain but powerfully simple sarcophagus in a niche in the cave wall. The **basilica**, an attractive late 19th-century edifice in pink limestone, has a wonderful mountain backdrop; it houses the Virgin of Covadonga and is surprisingly unadorned inside; the focus is on a replica of the Asturian victory cross forged by Pelayo to commemorate the victory. There's also a **museum** ① *Wed-Mon 1030-1400, 1600-1830 (1930 summer); €3*, on site, which primarily displays a collection of expensive gifts lavished on the Virgin over the years. On the main road, a couple of kilometres short of the sanctuary, is a **tourist information office** ① *T985 846 135, open Jul-Oct Mon-Sat 1000-1400, 1600-1900, Sun 1000-1400*.

Beyond Covadonga, a 12-km road leads further into the mountains, offering a couple of spectacular panoramas to the north. At the top are two lakes, **Enol** and **Ercina**, neither particularly appealing in themselves, but in superb surroundings bristling with peaks that are often snow capped. From Ercina, a 10-minute walk beyond Enol, there are some good walks: one heads south up the face of the Reblagas to an isolated *refugio*, Vega de Ario (six hours return); others head westwards and south to various viewpoints and *refugios*. A small information centre at the lake is open in summer and has reasonable maps of the area; otherwise grab them in Cangas.

Arenas de Cabrales and around → *For listings, see pages 55-58.*

The road east from Cangas to Arenas de Cabrales is very attractive, and there are numerous hamlets both on and off the road that offer potentially relaxing rural stays. There are too many lodging options to even begin to list; try the Asturian tourism website, www.infoasturias.com, or one of the most popular *casa rural* booking pages, www.toprural.com.

The **Arenas de Cabrales Valley** and the surrounding hillsides are famous throughout Spain for the strong blue cheese made here; *cabrales*. If you've been underwhelmed by Spanish cheeses so far, you're in for a treat. Not for nothing is the stuff known as the 'Spanish Roquefort'; it shares many similarities in taste and production methods with that classic French blue cheese. It's made from cows' milk, often with a percentage of sheep or

Picos de Europa

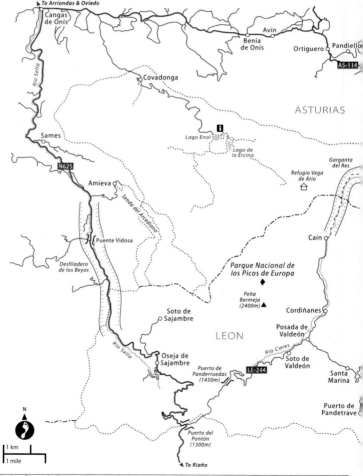

goat milk added, and is matured in damp caves, where the bacteria that give it its sharp taste and distinctive colour develop.

Arenas is a busy place, as it's here that many people cut south into the heart of the Picos around Poncebos and Sotres. It makes a good base for the region, with banks, restaurants, shops and plenty of hotels. There's a small tourist kiosk by the bridge.

In **Cares**, a five-minute walk across the bridge south of Arenas, the **Cueva del Cares** ⓘ *Apr-Oct daily 1000-1400, 1600-2000, Nov-Mar weekends only; €3*, is a small factory and

cave where Cabrales cheese is made in the traditional manner. A guided tour takes visitors through the process and finishes up with a tasting of the blue-blooded stuff.

Into the mountains → *For listings, see pages 55-58.*

Hiking the Cares Gorge trail

An hour's walk south of Arenas, the road reaches **Puente Poncebos**, a small collection of buildings set among high, bleak mountains. There's a shared-jeep service running to here and Sotres from Arenas. Apart from the magnificent view of Naranjo de Bulnes from the hamlet of Camarmeña, 1.5 km above Poncebos, the main reason people come here is to ascend the funicular to Bulnes or to walk the Cares Gorge, one of the Picos's most popular trails. It's about three hours from here to **Caín**, at the other end of the gorge; there's accommodation there, or you can continue another two hours to **Posada de Valdeón** (see page 64), if you don't meet up with a jeep that connects those two towns. This is the best direction to walk in, it gets more spectacular as you go, and Posada de Valdeón is a welcoming place to finish up.

The trail is there thanks to a hydroelectric scheme, and it follows the course of a small, fast-flowing canal that would itch for a fairground-style dinghy ride if it didn't plunge underground every few metres. It's not the best walk if you don't like heights or enclosed spaces; there are several claustrophobic tunnels (a torch helps) and the path runs alongside steep drops to the river much of the time. It's incredibly popular, so don't do it at weekends or in high summer unless you fancy a conga-line experience. From Poncebos, the trail climbs moderately for the first hour or so, leaving the river far below. If you hear jangling far above, it comes from belled goats, who seem to reach completely impossible locations high on the precipitous rocks.

The walk gets prettier and more dramatic as you approach the tail of the **Valdeón Valley**; the massive slabs of rock get bigger and more imposing, but provide shelter for a large range of tree and plant life. You'll probably see vultures circling lazily overhead and you may spot wallcreepers thumbing their beaks at gravity as they hop up perpendicular stone faces. After two hours or so, you'll reach a large green bridge; the path gently descends from here to Caín, crossing the river a couple more times. There are swimming holes here to refresh you, although the water is never less than icy. ▸▸ *See the Leonese Picos section, page 64, for Caín and beyond.*

Bulnes

Another walk from Poncebos is the steep hour-and-a-bit climb to Bulnes, a remote village in the midst of lofty mountains. Until 2001, this was the only way to get to the place, and villagers lugged their provisions up this trail as part of everyday life. There's now a **funicular railway** ① *runs every 30 mins 1000-1230, 1400-1800, €15.80/19.90 single/return, free for the villagers of Bulnes*, which climbs a steep 2.2 km through a tunnel from Poncebos to Bulnes, a controversial scheme that outraged environmentalists but pleased the villagers no end (although it certainly wasn't built for their benefit). The walk leaves from near the car park for the Cares Gorge walk, and crosses the river before zigzagging steeply up the hill. The first half is the hardest, but the trail continues to climb before reaching Bulnes.

Bulnes is magnificent, set in a breathtaking valley between towering grey peaks but with enough pasture land to sustain a grazing economy. The picturesque stone buildings, tolling of cowbells, and absence of cars makes it a supremely relaxing place. There are some seven permanent (and chatty) residents, though this is augmented at weekends and in summer. There are two separate hamlets. The lower one (La Villa) is some 300 m above the funicular station, and the higher ('El Castillo') another 10 minutes' climb. With the funicular's advent, there are now several places to stay and a few simple places to eat, most of which only open summer and weekends. From La Villa, a short uphill walk will take you to a viewpoint with magnificent vistas of the Naranjo de Bulnes mountain.

Hiking from Poncebos to Sotres
From Poncebos, a spectacular road winds through the brooding mountains to the remote village of Sotres (this route is also serviced by shared jeeps in season), another walking base. Sotres is slightly on the grim side, especially in bleak weather, but there are a couple of good lodging and eating options.

Hiking from Sotres to Vego de Urriello
One of the best walks from Sotres is the 4½ hours to the *refugio* of **Vega de Urriello** ① *T985 925 200; year-round*, in a grassy meadow near the signature peak of **Naranjo de Bulnes**, which is basically a massive rock jutting out from the massif; it's not a climb for the inexperienced. The walk to the *refugio* crosses the pass at **Pandébano**, from where there are excellent views. The *refugio* offers dorm accommodation (€10) and meals (€14).

East to Panes
Panes itself isn't worth a stop; it is characterized by a modern bridge in rusted iron and a 19th-century church topped by a tacky pastel-blue Jesus. From here, the N621 heads into Cantabria, heading north to the coast at Unquera, or winding south towards Potes along the spectacular **Desfiladero de la Hermida**.

Asturian Picos listings

For sleeping and eating price codes and other relevant information, see pages 13-19.

☺ Where to stay

Cangas de Onís *p50*
There are numerous places to stay – even in summer there should be space. The tourist office has a full list. Most are great value off-season. Among them are numerous *casas rurales*; check www.toprural.com.

€€€ Parador de Cangas de Onís, Villanueva s/n, T985 849 402, www.parador. es. Set in an old Benedictine monastery 3 km north of Cangas, this new parador offers excellent comfort and good views. Most of the rooms are in a modern annexe; those in the original building are less comfortable but more atmospheric.

€€€-€€ Hotel Nochendi, C Constantino González 4, T985 849 513, www.hotel nochendi.com. Stylish and comfortable, this small hotel has staff who appreciate your presence, and a good location on the river. It gets the gold medal for centre-of-town choices.

€€ Hotel Imperión/Puente Romano, C Puente Romano s/n, T985 849 339, www.hotelimperion.com. An authentically heavily decorated 19th-century mansion across the Sella, with courteous management and comfortable, if worn, heated rooms.

€€ Hotel La Plaza, C La Plaza 7, T985 848 308. Simple and cheery rooms with bathroom. The best have a balcony and look out towards the mountains.

€€ Hotel Los Lagos, Jardines de Ayuntamiento 3, T985 849 277, www.arceahoteles. com. Right on the main square, offering fair prices, upbeat and professional staff, and reasonable rooms that could do with a facelift. Comfortable beds and decent facilities including a sunny café downstairs, and a free internet terminal. Wi-Fi is extra.

€ Pensión Reconquista, Av Covadonga 6, T985 848 275. Modern, 6th-floor rooms with balconies overlooking the town, and that rarest of beasts, a good shower. Run out of the bar on the corner. An excellent option.

Around Cangas *p50*
€€ **El Rexacu**, Bobia de Arriba s/n, T985 844 303, www.elrexacu.com. Closes Mon-Wed from Oct-May. A reader alerted us to this excellent rural hotel in a village 18 km east of Cangas. It's a welcoming, nothing-too-much-trouble sort of place, and has fabulous views. There's a sociable lounge with books, games, and films, and the restaurant serves up excellent food, including home-grown veggies and even ostrich meat from the farm. Recommended.

Covadonga *p51*
€€€ **Gran Hotel Pelayo**, Covadonga s/n, T985 846 061, www.arceahoteles.com. Right in the middle of the complex at Covadonga, the Pelayo is devoid of warmth but is reasonably well equipped, with a good restaurant. The price halves off-season.
€€ **Casa Priena**, T985 846 070. Very close to the Covadonga sanctuary, this little *casa rural* offers 4 cute rooms decked out in fresh and cheerful colours. There's good walking from the doorstep (upwards) and the friendly owners rent out quad bikes.
€€ **Los Texos**, La Riera, T985 846 138, www.lostexos.com. A cosy stonebuilt rural hotel in the roadside village of La Riera, on the road to Covadonga and by the busy stream of the same name. Good value, attractive rooms in a great village location (once the traffic has died down in the evening).

Camping
Covadonga, T985 940 097, www.camping-covadonga.com. A bland campsite 4 km east of Cangas, at Soto by the main road.

Arenas de Cabrales and around *p51*
€€ **El Torrejón**, Arenas de Cabrales s/n, T985 846 428, www.eltorrejon.com. A cordial welcome and bargain prices await at this attractive rural hotel tucked away just off the main road in Arenas. There are fine views from some of the stylish rooms and a quaint garden to relax in.
€€ **Hotel Torrecerredo**, Barrio Los Llambriosos s/n, T985 846 640, www.hotel torrecerredo.com. About 500 m west of the centre of Arenas, this hotel is a breath of fresh air. Plenty of space, welcoming, humorous owners, and numerous activities; it makes a great base. Add to that great breakfasts and evening meals, and you have an excellent package.
€€ **Picos de Europa**, Ctra General s/n, T985 846 491, www.hotelpicosdeeuropa. com. A little faded but still Arenas's grandest hotel, with a swimming pool, rooms with great views and an *hórreo* (granary) by the bar in the garden.
€€ **Villa de Cabrales**, Ctra General s/n, T985 846 719, www.hotelcabrales.com. In a big stone building, this is a more modern affair, with smart rooms with balconies (although there's some traffic noise). The off-season rates here are appealing.

Camping
Camping Naranjo de Bulnes, Ctra Cangas–Panes Km 32.6, T985 846 578, open Mar-Oct. A 10-min walk east along the main road. They have bungalows available year-round.

Hiking the Cares Gorge trail *p54*
€€€ **El Mirador de Cabrales**, Poncebos, T985 846 673, www.arceahoteles.com. Open Mar-Sep. The top accommodation option in Poncebos, this attractive place offers a great location and decent restaurant. It's a little overpriced in the height of summer, when there's a 3-night minimum stay.
€€ **Hostal Poncebos**, Poncebos, T985 846 447, hostalponcebos@wanadoo.es. Dwarfed by mountains, this bright orange building sits right on the crystal-clear rushing Cares, and has reasonable rooms and a restaurant. They'll do a packed lunch for walkers for €5.

€ Garganta del Cares, Poncebos, T985 846 463. A comfortable *hostal* above a bar with en suite rooms that are heated and good value except in the height of summer (**€€**).

Bulnes *p54*
€€ La Casa del Chiflón, T985 845 943. In the lower village of Bulnes, this is a cosy mountain retreat with wooden beams and solid stone walls. Apart from a walkers' hostel, it's currently the only place to stay in Bulnes. It's a great base for hiking and should be booked ahead in summer.

Sotres *p55*
€€ Casa Cipriano, T985 945 024, www.casacipriano.com. A convivial mountain *hostal*, which runs many guided excursions in the area. The rooms are good, and there's a bar and restaurant.
€ La Perdiz, T985 945 011, www.laperdiz sotres.com. Opposite **Casa Cipriano**, has good rooms with bath.
€ Peña Castil, T985 945 070. Closed early Nov-Mar. A convivial stone walkers' hostel, this is a good base for hiking and has simple but clean bunks and a restaurant with a sunny terrace.

❷ Restaurants

Cangas de Onís *p50*
There are several cracking *sidrerías* (cider bars) that are excellent eating and drinking options.
€€€ Casa Marcial, La Salgar s/n, T985 840 991, www.casamarcial.com. This is perhaps the finest restaurant in rural Asturias. Nacho Manzano, the chef, has carved a great reputation for himself by blending rustic Asturian cooking traditions with modern technique and modish innovations. The results are spectacularly tasty. You'll find this cosy rustic stone house in the hills up a spectacular road some 6 km north of the town of Arriondas.
€€ El Abuelo, Av Covadonga 29, T985 848 733, www.elabuelocangasdeonis.com. A cheerful, warming restaurant specializing

in hearty stews and *fabadas*. There's a pleasant covered terrace in summer, and a top-value €10 lunch menu that'll leave you wholly satisfied. Recommended.
€€ El Molín de la Pedrera, C Bernabé Pendas 1, T985 849 109. A smart cider bar with some great fishy stews, as well as roast chestnuts in season. One of Cangas's best. The typically Asturian stew, *fabada*, is another top thing to try here.
€€ La Cueva, C Turismo 3, T985 947 775. Though the grotto is made of plastic, this *sidrería* behind the tourist office is an attractive place, and has plenty of tables to sit at and enjoy the outrageously proportioned *raciones*. Calamari, salads, and octopus are all recommendable.
€€ Mesón El Puente Romano, Av Covadonga s/n, T985 848 110. Come for the terrace looking at the medieval bridge. Simple but reasonable Asturian fare, including *fabada*.
€€ Sidrería Los Arcos, Av Covadonga 17, T985 849 277. Though the bar isn't as atmospheric as others, the tables host some of the town's better food. Great quality *raciones* of some fairly classy fare are the reason to come.
€ El Corchu, C Angel Tárano 5, T985 849 477. Near the church, this is an unpretentious traditional *sidrería*. The nearby **Potesu** is another more than sound option.

Arenas de Cabrales and around *p51*
€€ La Panera, C General s/n, T985 846 810. It's a good spot for a quiet drink, but the food is attractive too. There are plenty of dishes making full use of *cabrales* cheese; try it with wild mushrooms. Heavier dishes include Asturian Picos favourites like *fabada* or *cabrito asado* (roast goat).
€ La Cabraliega, C El Parque s/n, T985 846 681. Just off the main road on the way to Poncebos, this cosy spot is part shop, selling plenty of local cheeses, and part bar, with a little sunny terrace and various tapas making good use of local products.

€ **San Telmo**, Ctra General s/n, T985 846 505, gets plenty of tourists on its roadside terrace, but the food is great; try the ultimate expression of *cabrales*, chips 'n' cheese.

Bulnes *p54*
€€ **Bar Bulnes**, Bulnes, T985 845 934. Open weekends and summer. In the heart of the lower village, with a cosy bar serving up simple tapas and huge *bocadillos*, and a popular upstairs *comedor* doing elaborate plates, including *cabrito* and meat dishes.

🎵 Bars and clubs

Cangas de Onís *p50*
Mantra, C Turismo 3. The blend of Buddhas and Moroccan art is curious, but it's a peaceful place to sip on a variety of tasty herbal teas or have a post-dinner *copa*.

✴ Festivals

Cangas de Onís *p50*
25 Jul The Fiesta de **Santiago** is celebrated with gusto at Cangas de Onís. On the same day, the **Fiesta del Pastor** is a big party with shepherds and visitors mixing on the shores of Lake Enol near Covadonga.
Aug Regattas down the Río Sella from Arriondas. This **Descenso de la Sella** features everyone from canoeists to professional partiers. The fiesta starts in Arriondas and ends in Ribadesella amid boisterous scenes. One of the region's most memorable events.
8 Sep The Picos' biggest day is **Asturias Day**, the feast of the Virgen de Covadonga, celebrated with processions and partying.

🛍 Shopping

Cangas de Onís *p50*
La Barata, Av Covadonga 13, T985 848 027. An attractive shop dealing in Asturian handicrafts, deli produce and souvenirs.

🏃 What to do

Cangas de Onís *p50*
Aquassport, C Juan Carlos I 26, T985 840 364, www.aquassport.com. A popular canoeing and quad-biking operator based in Arriondas itself, with good facilities and decent prices for combined activities.
Cangas Aventura, Bernabé Pendas 2, T985 849 261, www.cangasaventura. com. Canoeing trips on the river and quad excursions into the mountains.
Escuela Asturiana de Piragüismo, C Turista 6, T985 841 282, www.piraguismo. com. Near the tourist office in Cangas, they organize canoeing trips on the Río Sella as well as horse riding and canyoning.
K2 Aventura, Las Rozas s/n, T985 849 358, www.k2aventura.com. A canoeing outfit based on the river between Arriondas and Cangas. There's a bar on hand for *après-kayak* ciders.

⊖ Transport

Cangas de Onís *p50*
Bus Cangas de Onís is serviced very regularly by **ALSA** buses from **Oviedo** and **Gijón** (almost hourly; 1 hr 20 mins).

Covadonga *p51*
Bus From **Oviedo** and **Cangas**, 4 buses a day ascend to Covadonga. In summer a couple a day continue to the lakes; about 4 a day continue along the AS114 to **Arenas de Cabrales** and **Panes**.

Arenas de Cabrales and around *p51*
Bus There are 4 ALSA buses a day from **Cangas de Onís** and **Oviedo** to **Panes** via Arenas de Cabrales. From Arenas, ALSA run buses to the Bulnes funicular at **Poncebos**. Shared-jeep taxis also do this trip in summer, and continue to **Sotres**.

Cantabrian Picos

This is the most visited section of the Picos due to its easy road access and good tourist facilities. The region's main centre is the town of Potes, a very attractive place, gouged in half by its river. The heart of the area is the Liébana Valley, a green swathe watered by mountain streams and the Río Deva. It's noted for its cheeses, its chestnuts and its *orujo*, a fiery grape spirit that comes in original form as well as more mellow, flavoured varieties. A hefty shot in a cup of black coffee is another popular way of taking it. West of Potes, the road winds up to the spectacular natural theatre of Fuente Dé, starting point for plenty of memorable walks.

Potes and around → *For listings, see pages 61-63.*

Potes is a gorgeous little town on the side of a hill by the Río Deva, with cobbled streets and a few noble stone buildings (those that survived the Civil War damage). The most striking of these is a large tower, looking like a medieval fort, but in fact built as a mansion by the Marqués de Santillana in the 16th century; it's now the town hall. Another tower nearby holds changing exhibitions. Potes makes the best base in this part of the Picos, although in summer it struggles to accommodate the numbers passing through; there's an unbroken line of cars winding through its centre.

There are several banks and supermarkets in town, as well as a petrol station. In the bus station (worth a visit for its painstakingly detailed relief model of the Picos region) is the town's **tourist office** ① *summer daily 1000-1400, 1600-2000, winter Mon, Thu-Sat 1000-1400, 1600-1800, Sun 1000-1400*. More information is available 4 km north of town in Tama at the **Sotama visitor centre** ① *T942 738 109, Oct-Jun daily 0900-1800, Jul-Sep 0900-2000*, a striking, eco-friendly, wood-clad building with an environmental exhibition and national park information office. If you're going to do some walking in the area, make sure you pick up a proper map from one of these places. Even on the brightest of days, mists can descend rapidly, and in any event some trails are ambiguously marked.

A 45-minute walk from Potes, off the Fuente Dé road, is a monastery of great importance, **Monasterio de Santo Toribio de Liébana** ① *daily 1000-1300, 1600-1900*. Although in a magnificent setting, the building itself isn't of massive interest, but makes up for it with two claims to fame. The first is that it was here that the Abbot Beatus de Liébana wrote his apocalyptic commentaries on the book of Saint John; one of the superb illustrated copies of this work is kept here, far from the public gaze (see box, page 60). Prints of some of the pages of this beautiful work are displayed around the cloister (you may recognize some from the film *The Name of the Rose*), and there are some good laminates on sale for €2 in the shop. The other item of interest here is kept in a side chapel off the main church. It is nothing less than the largest fragment of the True Cross in existence, a hefty chunk of cypress wood that measures 63 cm x 40 cm and has one of the nail-holes. It's embedded in an ornate silver Gothic crucifix.

Beatus and a medieval bestseller

In the middle of the eighth century when the future of Christianity in Europe was in the balance, a monk writing in the remote mountains of Cantabria produced a work that was to be the equivalent of a European bestseller for the next 400 years. Writing from the monastery of Liébana, Beatus wrote a commentary on Saint John's Apocalypse that struck a note with readers who, as well as fearing further invasions from the Moors, also believed that the approaching millennium would bring the coming of the Antichrist. Monasteries across Northern Spain began to produce beautifully illustrated copies of the monk's work. The quality of the illustrations make these manuscripts, known as *beatos*, masterpieces of medieval art. The one in Burgo de Osma, for example, has been described as "the most beautiful book in the world". Only 22 of these manuscripts still survive, nearly all of them in academic libraries.

Umberto Eco used the Beatus manuscripts as the basis for his novel *The Name of the Rose*. However, if you fancy reading the original for yourself be warned: Eco describes the Beatus text as "tortuous, even to those well acquainted with medieval Latin".

West of Potes to Fuente Dé → *For listings, see pages 61-63.*

The N621 follows the Río Deva upstream to the west of Potes, passing through several pretty hamlets. It's a well-travelled route, but just off the main road there are some pretty tranquil *casas rurales* where you can stay.

The road stops at Fuente Dé, and it's not hard to see why; there's a massive semicircle of rock ahead; a spectacular natural wall that rises 800 m and is almost sheer. It is named Fuente Dé because this is where the Deva springs from the ground, but there's little here apart from two hotels, a campsite and a cable-car station. The **cable car** ① *T942 736 610, www.cantur.com, daily 1000-1800, 0900-2000 in summer, €9.10 one way/€15.15 return*, takes 3½ minutes to trundle to the top of the rocky theatre; it's a bad one for claustrophobes, as you're jammed with 25 or so others into the tiny capsule. Expect a long wait in summer. It usually closes for a couple of weeks in February.

Hiking around Fuente Dé → *See map, page 52.*

There are some superb walks in this area, some leaving from the top cable-car station; don't worry if you don't fancy the trip up, as there's a steep path that'll get you there eventually. At the top station, there's an unremarkable tourist complex and the start of a jagged, rocky plateau, an Alpine landscape in contrast to the lush meadows below. In clear weather the views from here are magnificent, with the parador hardly more than a dot below. Following the track from here, you'll soon leave the crowds behind and start a gentle ascent to the top of a rise. Descending to the right from here, you'll come to the **Refugio de Aliva** (see page 62), a year-round hotel and *albergue*. From here, a spectacular 1½-hour descent winds around the valley and down to its floor at Espinama, from where you can follow the river back up to Fuente Dé. The whole circuit takes about four hours and is one of the most beautiful walks in the Picos. Other walks start from the campsite and provide equally spectacular valley and mountain views.

North towards Panes

North of Potes, the N621 heads into Asturias towards Panes through the very narrow gorge of La Hermida. At **Lebeña**, 500 m off the road through the gorge, and 8 km from Potes, is a worthwhile church, **Iglesia de Santa María de Lebeña** ① *Tue-Sat 1000-1330, 1600-1900, Sun 1100-1400, €2*, set against a superb backdrop of massive rock. Founded in the 10th century, its interior is Mozarabic, with horseshoe arches on a rectangular ground plan. It's a beautifully simple space; most interesting is the altarstone, carved with a series of circles deemed to represent nature, the heavens and the redemptive power of Christ; symbols that go back to the Visigoths and beyond.

South to León

South from Potes, the road winds through the green **Liébana Valley** for a while, then begins to ascend to the **Puerto San Glorio** and **León** province. This stretch of road offers perhaps the best views in the entire Picos; the contrast between the lush green valley and the harsh grey mountains is superb.

Cantabrian Picos listings

For sleeping and eating price codes and other relevant information, see pages 13-19.

◉ Where to stay

Potes and around *p59*
€€ Casa Cayo, C Cántabra 6, T942 730 150, www.casacayo.com. Closed Feb. A very good option above Potes' best bar and restaurant. The rooms are large, comfortable and tastefully furnished; some overlook the river. Recommended.
€€ La Casa de las Chimeneas, Plaza Mayor s/n, Tudes, T942 736 300, www.la casadelaschimeneas.es. Some 9 km south of Potes off the Riaño road, this excellent complex of independent rustic apartments is a great base for exploring the Liébana valleys. The 7 apartments are all different, and charmingly decorated, with designs taken from the Beatus manuscript at the Toribio monastery. There's often a 3-day minimum stay, rising to 1 week in Jul-Aug. The owners speak English.
€€ Posada La Antigua, C Cántabra 9, T942 730 037, posadalaantigua@mixmail. com. Set above and behind a shop in the old part of town, this has rooms with plenty of character at a fairly decent price. Some aren't very spacious, but they are

comfortable, and have efficient heating and a/c. The best rooms are on the top floor, with balustraded balconies.
€ Hostal Coriscao, C La Serna s/n, T942 730 458. A simple but friendly and cheap option by the car park on the west side of the river. Rooms are basic, with shared bathroom, and can be chilly in winter.

Camping
Camping La Viorna, T942 732 021, www.campinglaviorna.com. On the road to the Santo Toribio monastery just a 15-min walk from the centre of Potes, this is a good campsite in a pleasant setting with swimming pools.

West of Potes to Fuente Dé *p60*
€€€ Parador de Fuente Dé, Fuente Dé, T942 736 651, www.parador.es. Open Mar-Oct. The top place to stay. A modern but fairly sensitive building, this is one of the cheaper paradors but loses nothing on location, particularly when the day trippers have gone home. The rooms are spacious and attractive, most with views of some sort, and the restaurant focuses on Picos cuisine.
€€ Hotel del Oso, Cosgaya s/n, T942 733 018, www.hoteldeloso.com. One of numerous accommodation choices along

the road between Potes and Fuente Dé, this stylish rural hotel appeals for its fine restaurant and smart, colourful rooms, many of which have balconies from which to appreciate the views and enjoy the mountain air.

€€ Rebeco, Fuente Dé, T942 736 601, www.hotelrebeco.com. Cheaper than the parador, with plenty of comfort despite smallish rooms, as well as a bar/restaurant. It's not de luxe, but the location makes up for it.

Camping
Camping El Redondo, T942 736 699, www.elredondopicosdeeuropa.com. 5 mins' walk past the cable car in Fuente Dé, this campsite also has bunkbed accommodation (but only 20 places) and is at the start of walking trails.

Hiking around Fuente Dé *p60*
€€ Refugio de Aliva, T942 730 999, www.cantur.com. Open Mid-Jun to Oct. Atop the plateau, this hotel and hostel (**€**) is a memorable place to stay, and a wonderful base for walks. It has a popular restaurant (popular because there's a jeep running from the top of the cable-car station) that does a *menú del día* for €15.

Restaurants

Potes and around *p59*
€€ Asador Llorente, C San Roque 1, T942 738 165. This restaurant has fast become a local favourite, so you'll want to book ahead. The warm rustic *comedor* sits right on the top floor, under the old building's beamed roof, and serves good-value meats and other traditional dishes.
€€ Casa Cayo, C Cántabra 6, T942 730 150. Closed Feb. Potes's best option, very lively and cheerful with huge portions. The *cocidos* (chickpea and pork stews) are good, as are the the *revueltos* (scrambled eggs mixed with everything). Some tables overlook the river.

€€ El Bodegón, C San Roque 14, T942 730 247. Atmospheric and with most friendly service, this attractive restaurant is set in a stone building off an old-timers' bar. It's a good place to tuck into a hearty *cocido lebaniego* (the local chickpea stew garnished with sausage and pork). *Revuelto de erizos* (scrambled egg with sea-urchins) is also delicious, but an acquired taste.
€ Los Camachos, C El Llano, T942 732 148. Cheap, decent food in a lively Cantabrian bar that has won prizes for its home-made *orujo*.
€ Tasca Cántabra, C Cántabra s/n, T942 730 714. A pleasing no-frills option with an upstairs *comedor*. In winter, try the *alubias con jabalí* (beans with wild boar), a real belly warmer for a pittance.

✺ Festivals

Potes and around *p59*
2 Jul Romería (pilgrimage procession) and festival in the Liébana Valley.
1st week in Nov Orujo festival in Potes; can be messy.

⚙ What to do

Potes and around *p59*
Europicos, C San Roque 6, Potes, T942 730 724, www.europicos.com. Organizes everything from quad tours or 4WD trips to paragliding. Mountain bikes from €20 for a ½-day.
La Rodrigona, Cillorigo de Liébana s/n, Tama, T615 970 442, www.larodrigona.com. Horse-trekking operator based in a village north of Potes near the Sotama information centre.
Picos Awentura, C Cervantes 3, Potes, T942 732 161, www.lacasadelascosas.com. By the bridge in Potes, this friendly bunch offer climbing and walking activities in the area, as well as paragliding, horse riding and canoeing.
Potes Tur, C San Roque 19, Potes, T942 732 164, www.potestur.es. Specialize in quad trips into the mountains, also other options.

Transport

Potes and around *p59*

Bus 3 buses a day from **Santander** to Potes, stopping along the western Cantabrian coast, turning inland at **Unquera**, and stopping at **Panes**. This connects with 2 of 3 daily buses from Potes to the cablecar at **Fuente Dé**.

Leonese Picos

Although this part of the Picos range isn't as endowed with tourist facilities as the Asturian or Cantabrian sections, it contains much of the area's most dramatic scenery, with breathtaking mountain vistas suddenly revealed as you round a bend in the path or road. It's also colder and, in winter snowier, than the more northern sections. While Riaño is the area's biggest town, it's a bit far from the action and not especially charming; a better bet is little Posada de Valdeón, spectacularly set in a lush valley surrounded by rocky peaks.

South to the Naranco Valley

The N621 running south from Potes winds its way upwards through lush alpine meadows before meeting León province at the spectacular **Puerto de San Glorio Pass**, where plans for a controversial ski station have been put on hold pending a lengthy environmental review. Descending rapidly through dark rocks and grassy pasture, the first settlement is **Llánaves de la Reina**.

Valdeón Valley → *For listings, see pages 65-66.*

Santa Marina

Some 6 km further south is the turn-off for the Valdeón Valley (you can also access it west of Riaño via a wider, faster road), the main part of the Leonese Picos and a remote rural area famous for its strong blue soft cheese. The road climbs to the **Puerto de Pandetrave** at 1562 m, which suddenly reveals a superb view of the valley, dwarfed by the imposing stone masses of the Picos. The first village in the valley itself is Santa Marina, a very rural settlement of simple stone houses. It's a friendly village with a good campsite and a hostel.

Posada de Valdeón

Four kilometres further up the lovely grassy valley is the area's main settlement, Posada de Valdeón. This is the southern terminus for the popular walk along the Cares Gorge (see page 54), and is well equipped for such a small place, with hotels, a supermarket and bank, but no cash machine. The setting is spectacular, with the intimidating mass of **Peña Bermeja** behind it contrasting with the lush pasturelands around.

The Picos de Europa National Park has an **information office** ① *T987 740 504, Mon-Fri 0900-1700, Wed 1400-1700 only*, in Posada from where it runs free guided trips during the summer months (phone for details). There are several places to stay.

Caín

North from Posada de Valdeón, a steep and narrow road makes its way to the village of Caín, a walk of just over 1½ hours. Jeeps run a shared-taxi service between the two towns. Not far from Posada, a fantastic view opens up as the valley seems to be swallowed up by lofty mountains; it's an awe-inspiring sight in good weather. The **Mirador de Pombo** is one vantage point to appreciate the vista; it's marked by a slender chamois and a confusing diagram of the peaks around. Before you reach here, the hamlet of **Cordiñanes** has a good rustic *pensión*.

Caín itself would be about as isolated as a rural village gets were it not for the number of walkers passing through the **Garganta de Cares**. As it is, there are a couple of restaurants, shops and a few lodging options.

West to Asturias
From Posada de Valdeón, the LE244 runs west over the Panderruedas Pass to meet the main N625 near the windy Puerto de Pontón Pass a few kilometres west of Riaño. Continuing northwards, the road enters the maw of the **Desfiladero de los Beyos**, a narrow gorge framed by massive rockfaces; a haunt of vultures and anglers that winds its way into Asturias.

Leonese Picos listings

For sleeping and eating price codes and other relevant information, see pages 13-19.

● Where to stay

Santa Marina *p64*
€€ Casa Friero, C Amapolas 1, T987 742 658. A very good, if slightly pricey, *casa rural* in the village; kitchen facilities are available for guests' use. Sleeps 6 and is only available as an entire rental; €90 per day or €420 for a week.
€ La Ardilla Real, Plaza de la Esquina, T987 742 677, www.alberguelaardillareal.com. A friendly place in the heart of the village that offers simple but comfortable dormitory accommodation (€12 per person) and warming home-style meals.

Camping
Camping El Cares, 1 km out of town, T987 742 676. A campsite where you can rent horses to explore the valley.

Posada de Valdeón *p64*
€€ Posada El Asturiano, Ctra Cordiñanes s/n, T987 740 514. A favourite with many Picos regulars, this has warm and comfortable rooms just off the square and a reasonable restaurant. It's not quite so inviting in winter, when it feels a bit abandoned and musty.

€ Ezkurra, Plaza Cortina Concejo s/n, T987 740 547. A stay at this warm and welcoming *casa rural* feels like sleeping at a friend's place rather than staying at a hotel. There's plenty of comfort at very low prices, and good information from the hospitable owner. Breakfast is delicious and features home-made *bizcocho*.
€ Hostal Campo, Ctra Cordiñanes s/n, T987 740 502. In the centre of the town, this friendly choice has big, warm and comfy rooms with modern bathrooms and views at a reasonable price. Fuel up for the hike with their delicious €4 breakfast.
€ Pensión Begoña, Plaza Cortina Concejo s/n, T987 740 516. Run by the same management as the **Hostal Campo**, this is a friendly option, cheap, fairly basic and likeable; rooms have clean shared bathroom and a down-to-earth walkers' vibe.

Camping
El Valdeón, T987 742 605. Open summer only. The closest campsite is a couple of kilometres out on the road to Soto.

Caín *p64*
€€ Posada del Montañero, Caín, T987 742 711. The nicest option, open Apr-Sep, a comfortable but overpriced inn with a good simple restaurant.
€ Casa Cuevas, Caín, T987 740 500, www.casacuevas.es. Recently refurbished,

this walkers' spot offers comfortable, if a touch spartan, rooms, and is the village's best spot for a no-frills feed. There's a *menú* for €10; otherwise ask for *cabrito asado*, roast goat that is the region's speciality.
€ Rojo, C Santiago 8, Cordiñanes, T987 740 523. A rustic *pensión*, clean and comfortable with an unbeatable location if you're not scared of big, powerful mountains.

🍴 Restaurants

Posada de Valdeón *p64*
€ Pensión Begoña, see Where to stay, above. Just about the best place to eat in the Leonese Picos, this simple mountain inn has fed ex-prime minister Zapatero and offers hospitable service and hearty no-frills traditional cooking. It's a set menu (€14) with limited choice – you might get trout, which abound in the streams around here, or stew made from freshly hunted boar or venison – but it's bound to be hearty and good.

✱ Festivals

Posada de Valdeón *p64*
Sep 8 The Leonese Picos's biggest day is the fiesta of the Virgen de Corona in the Valdeón Valley.

⊖ Transport

Posada de Valdeón *p64*
Bus The southern part of the Picos is a bit problematic when it comes to transport. There's 1 bus Mon-Fri from **León** to Posada de Valdeón, and on to **Caín**, currently leaving León at 1830. There are 5 buses to **Riaño** from León Mon-Fri, 2 on Sat, and 1 on Sun.

Taxi There's a shared taxi service from Posada de Valdeón to **Caín**, at the head of the Cares Gorge walk.

Contents

Footprint features

Asturias

Earthy Asturias has a different feel to much of Northern Spain. It's a land of mining, fishing and good cheer, exemplified by its superb cider culture – a legacy of the Celts. There are few more interesting places to have a drink than an Asturian sidrería, with sawdust-covered floor and streams of booze poured from alarming heights. Round off the experience with some of the province's great seafood and you'll be in gastro heaven.

Asturias has had the foresight to look after its natural heritage. While the province is heavily industrialized, there are vast swathes of untouched old-growth forest inland that still harbour bears and wolves. A well-documented network of trails gives access to these places, maintained by an enthusiastic army of ecologists.

The cities of the region are no less appealing. Oviedo, an elegant and beautiful capital, claims some of the best of the ancient pre-Romanesque architecture left by the Asturian monarchs; Gijón is a lively place with an excellent beach; while Avilés shields a beautifully preserved old town inside an unsightly ring of industry. The nearby airport offers direct budget flights to London.

Although the sea temperatures aren't exactly Caribbean and rain is never unlikely, it's not hard to see why the Asturian coast is so popular in summer: the mix of sandy beaches and pretty fishing ports is hard to beat. Hit the east coast for a more developed summer scene, or the west for some more low-key places.

Oviedo and around

Oviedo, the capital of Asturias, seems to have come a long way since Clarín, in his biting attack on 19th-century Spanish provincialism and hypocrisy, La Regenta, wrote in 1884, "he looked down on ... the old squashed and blackened dwellings; the vain citizens thought them palaces but they were burrows, caves, piles of earth, the work of moles". Nowadays, after an extensive programme of pedestrianization and restoration, the new town is a prosperous hive of shops and cafés, while old Oviedo is an extremely attractive web of plazas and old palaces built of honey-coloured stone. Three of the best and most accessible examples of the distinctive and beautiful Asturian pre-Romanesque style are to be found in and around Oviedo; other highlights include the cathedral, the Museo de Bellas Artes, and the numerous intriguing public sculptures around town. There is even a life-size statue of Woody Allen in Oviedo – but people keep stealing the glasses. In the local dialect, Bable, Oviedo is written and pronounced 'Uvieu'.

There's plenty to explore outside the city too. Many of the valleys south of Oviedo are pockmarked with coal mines, which are gradually being closed down. Towns to the west, such as Pravia, ancient Asturian capital, and Salas, hometown of an arch-inquisitor, can be easily visited as day trips from Oviedo or Gijón, although they also make good bases in themselves; there are several rewarding walks in the area. This is salmon country – in season, the rivers teem with them, and also with phalanxes of local and international fly-fishers.

Arriving in Oviedo → *Phone code: 985. B2. Population: 224,005.*

Getting there
Asturias's international airport (OVD) is 10 km west of Avilés, but is also connected by regular bus to Oviedo and Gijón. **easyJet** fly here directly from London Stansted and Geneva, and **Air Berlin** connect to Oviedo from many German and Austrian cities via their Mallorca hub. There are regular internal connections with Madrid and Barcelona with **Iberia** and **Spanair**.

Getting around
Buses are useful for reaching outlying areas – there are 12 or so routes, clearly labelled at bus stops. Taxis are easy to find, but bear in mind that, due to Oviedo's commitment to

pedestrianization, many locations aren't easily accessible by car. There are several central parking stations. Hemmed in by hills, Oviedo is a fairly compact city, and easy to walk around. From the bus and train stations it's a 15-minute walk to the heart of the old town down Calle Uría; most of the accommodation is closer to the centre.

Best time to visit

Oviedo has a comparatively mild climate; usually neither winter nor summer hits uncomfortable extremes, although it is notoriously rainy in autumn and winter. Oviedo's major fiesta is in September (see page 81), but the *sidrerías* (cider bars) and other haunts are busy year-round.

Tourist information

The Asturias regional **tourist office** ① *C Cimadevilla 4, T985 213 385, ofiturio@princast.es, Oct-Jun Mon-Sat 1000-1800, Jul-Sep Mon-Fri 1000-2000, Sat-Sun 1000-1900*, is conveniently central. The helpful **main municipal office** ① *Plaza de la Constitución 4, T984 086 060, turismo-oviedo@ayto-oviedo.es, daily Oct-May 1000-1400, 1630-1900, Jun 1000-1900, Jul-Sep 0930-1930*, is just down the road from here. There's a **smaller municipal office** ① *Campo de San Francisco park, T985 227 586, 0930-1400, 1630-1930*. There's also a tourist information desk in the bus station (same hours). The website www.infoasturias.com is a valuable resource run by the tourist board.

Background

Oviedo was born in the early years of the stubborn Asturian monarchy, when a monastery was founded on the hill of 'Ovetao' in the mid-eighth century. Successive kings added other buildings until Alfonso II saw the city's potential, rebuilt and expanded it, and moved his court here in AD 808. He saw it as a new Toledo (the former Christian capital having long since fallen to the Moors). It was this period that saw the consolidation of the pre-Romanesque style, as Alfonso commissioned an impressive series of buildings. A glorious century in the spotlight followed, but Oviedo soon returned to relative obscurity when the court was moved south to León. Oviedo continued to grow through the Middle Ages, however, partly as a result of pilgrim traffic to Santiago. The university was founded in about 1600, which helped to raise the city's profile. Real prosperity arrived with the Industrial Revolution and, crucially, the discovery of coal in the green valleys near the Asturian capital. Asturias became a stronghold of miner-driven unionism and socialism, and Oviedo suffered massive damage in the 1934 miners' revolt, and again in the Civil War. Franco had a long memory, and it's only fairly recently that Oviedo has emerged from his shadow. A progressive town council has transformed the city, embarking on a massive program of pedestrianization (there are over 80 pedestrian-only streets), restoration, and commissioning of public sculpture. Now, painted and scrubbed, Oviedo is taking new pride in living up to its coat of arms as the "very noble, very loyal, meritorious, unconquered, heroic, and good city of Oviedo".

Places in Oviedo

Cathedral

① *Nov-Feb Mon-Sat 1000-1300, 1600-1800, Mar-May and Oct Mon-Fri 1000-1300, 1600-1900, Sat 1000-1300, 1600-1800, Jun Mon-Fri 1000-1300, 1600-2000, Sat 1000-1300, 1600-1800, Jul-Sep Mon-Fri 1015-1915, Sat 1015-1715, admission to Cámara Santa, museum, and cloister €3.50, Cámara Santa only €2 (guided visit).*

The cathedral, a warmly-coloured and harmonious construction, dominates the **Plaza de Alfonso el Casto** with its delicate and exuberant spire. While most of the building is of 14th- and 15th-century design, it contains a series of important relics of the Asturian kings in its Cámara Santa. This chamber, originally part of Alfonso II's palace, contains the Cruz de los Angeles and the Cruz de la Victoria; the two emblematic, bejewelled crucifixes were gifts to the church by Kings Alfonso II and III respectively. The former is now the symbol of Oviedo, while the latter features on the Asturian coat of arms. Also behind glass in the Cámara Santa is a silver ark containing relics perhaps brought from the Holy Land to Spain in the seventh century. One of the relics, supposedly the shroud of Christ, is behind a panel in the back wall; it is brought out and venerated three times a year. The ark itself contains a bumper crop including a piece of the true cross, some bread from the Last Supper, part of Christ's clothing, some of his nappies, and milk of the Virgin Mary. The cathedral also has an attractive cloister and a museum with a good collection of objects, although these are left to the visitor's interpretation. Across the square from the cathedral is a statue of Clarín's *La Regenta*.

Museo Arqueológico
ⓘ *C San Vicente, Tue-Sat 1000-1330, 1600-1800, Sun 1100-1300, free. Currently under renovation; should be open for summer 2011.*
Behind the cathedral is the museum of archaeology, which is built around a beautiful monastery cloister. The sparsely labelled finds lack context, but it's a pleasant stroll around the old building.

Museo de las Bellas Artes de Asturias
ⓘ *Sep-Jun Tue-Fri 1030-1400, 1630-2030, Sat 1130-1400, 1700-2000, Sun 1130-1430; Jul and Aug Tue-Sat 1030-1400, 1630-2030, Sun 1030-1430; free.*
The fine arts museum is housed in a 17th-century palace and a grand 18th-century townhouse that are joined back-to-back. There are two entrances, one on Calle Santa Ana, and one on Calle Rúa. The museum has an excellent collection of 20th-century Asturian art and a good selection of Spanish masters. In the vestibule at the Santa Ana entrance hangs José Uría y Uría's tragic *Después de una huelga (After a Strike)*. Painted in 1895, it evocatively demonstrates that the events of 1934 and 1936 were a long time in the making.

Old town
The old town is made for wandering. The walk-through **Ayuntamiento** is on **Plaza de la Constitución**, as is the honey-coloured **Iglesia de San Isidoro**, still daubed with ancient graffiti, as graduating students traditionally painted their names there. Other pretty plazas include **Trascorrales**, and **Porlier**; the latter is home to the mysterious sculpture *El regreso de William B Arrensberg (The Return of William B Arrensberg)*, one of many street sculptures that invigorate Oviedo. From here, walk down Calle San Francisco (the Assisi saint passed through Oviedo on his way to Santiago) to the large park of the same name. *Maternidad*, a sculpture by the Colombian artist Fernando Botero, is an unmissable landmark here on the **Plaza de la Escandalera**; it's irreverently nicknamed *La Muyerona (The Big Woman)* by locals.

North of the old town
Heading north, **Calle Gascona**'s sharpish slope serves to drain away all the cider spilled in its numerous and gregarious *sidrerías*. The pre-Romanesque **Iglesia de San Julián de los Prados** ⓘ *T607 353 999, Oct-Apr Tue-Sat 0930-1130, May-Sep Tue-Fri 1000-1230, 1600-1730, Sat 0930-1200, 1530-1700; all year Mon 1000-1230 unguided; guided visits take 30 mins, last*

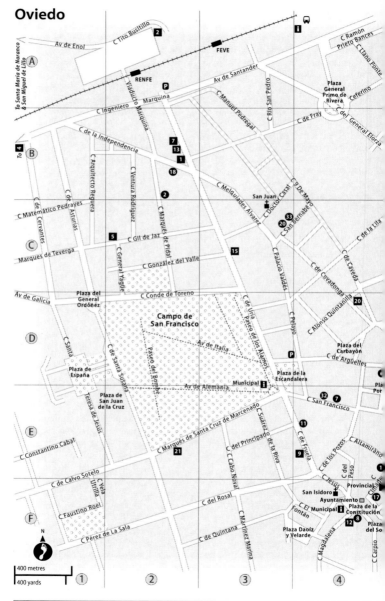

Oviedo

To Santa María de Naranco & San Miguel de Lillo

Av de Enol

C Tito Bustillo

FEVE

C Ramón Prieto Bances

C Llano Ponte

Ceferino

Plaza General Primo de Rivera

RENFE

Viaducto Marquina

C Ingeniero Marquina

Av de Santander

C Manuel Pedregal

C Río San Pedro

C de Fray

C del General Elorza

C de la Independencia

C Arquitecto Reguera

C de Levantes

C de Asturias

C Matemático Pedrayes

C Ventura Rodríguez

C Marqués de Pidal

C Melquíades Álvarez

C Doctor Casal

C 9 De Mayo

San Juan

C San Bernabé

C de la Lila

C Gil de Jaz

C González del Valle

C de Caveda

C Palacio Valdés

Marques de Teverga

C General Yagüe

C Conde de Toreno

Campo de San Francisco

C de Uría / Paseo de los Álamos

Av de Italia

Paseo del Bombé

C Pelayo

C de Covadonga

C Alonso Quintanilla

Plaza del Carbayón

Plaza del General Ordóñez

Av de Galicia

C Santa

C de Santa Susana

Plaza de España

Plaza de San Juan de la Cruz

Av de Alemania

Municipal

Plaza de la Escandalera

C de Argüelles

Teresa de Jesús

C San Francisco

C Fruela

C de Frivela

Plaza de la Constitución

C Constantino Cabal

C Marqués de Santa Cruz de Marcenado

C del Principado

C Suárez de la Riva

C de los Pozos

C del Peso

C Altamirano

C de Calvo Sotelo

C Cabo Noval

San Isidoro

Ayuntamiento

El Municipal

Provincial

C de la Utilla

C Faustino Roel

C del Rosal

C Martínez Marina

C Magdalena

Plaza Daoíz y Velarde

Plaza del Sol

C Pérez de La Sala

C de Quintana

C Carpio

N

400 metres
400 yards

entry 30 mins before closing time €1.20, Mon free*, was built by Alfonso II in the first half of the ninth century. Northeast of the old centre, beyond the fountained **Plaza de la Cruz Roja**, it now struggles for serenity beside the Gijón motorway. Designed with the characteristic triple nave, the highlight of the church is its superbly preserved frescoes.

Los Monumentos

ⓘ *Apr-Sep Tue-Sat 0930-1330, 1530-1930, Sun and Mon 0930-1330; Oct-Mar Tue-Sat 1000-1300, 1500-1700, Sun and Mon 1000-1300. Admission by tour only; €3, free Mon; last tour 30 mins before closing. Tour covers both buildings, so if no one seems to be around, wait; or check the other building. The guardian's phone number is T638 260 163.*

The pre-Romanesque structures of Santa María de Naranco and San Miguel de Lillo, collectively known as Los Monumentos, overlook the city on Naranco hill to the northwest. There's a good view over Oviedo, which, it has to be said, isn't super-attractive from up here, but is backed by beautiful mountains.

Santa María de Naranco, built as a palace by Ramiro I (1842-1850), is arguably the finest example of this architecture. The columns in the upper hall could almost be carved from bone or ivory, such is the skill of the stonework. Balconies at either end add to the lightness of the design; one contains an altar with an inscription of the king. A range of sculptural motifs, many of them depicting alarming animals, decorate the hall, and have been attributed to Visigothic and Byzantine influences. Underneath the hall is another chamber variously identified as a crypt, bathhouse, and servants' quarters.

The **Iglesia de San Miguel de Lillo**, a stone's throw further up the road, is a church also constructed during the reign of Ramiro I. What remains is a conglomeration of the original building – much of which collapsed in the 13th century – and later additions. The original building was undoubtedly an amazing structure for the time in which it

Asturian pre-Romanesque

From the late eighth century onwards, the rulers of the young Asturian kingdom began to construct religious and civil buildings in an original style that drew on Roman, Visigothic and Byzantine elements. Some of these buildings remain standing in Asturias, and provide a strikingly beautiful, not to mention unusual, architectural heritage.

Around 20 standing churches and halls around the province preserve some or many of their original features. The style was characterized by barrel-vaulted, usually triple naves and a rectangular or cross-shaped ground plan. The roof is supported by columns, often elaborately carved with motifs derived from Moorish and Byzantine models. The transepts are wide, and the altar area often raised. A triple apse is a common feature, sometimes divided from the rest of the building by a triple arch; the windows, too, are characteristic, divided by a miniature column. The exterior is typically buttressed; the supports line up with the interior columns.

The style progressed quickly and reached its peak in the mid-ninth century under king Ramiro I. From this period are the supreme examples outside Oviedo, Santa María de Naranco and San Miguel de Lillo. Other excellent example of the Asturian pre-Romanesque style (a term coined by Jovellanos), are San Salvador de Valdedios not far from Villaviciosa; San Julián de los Prados in Oviedo, and Santa Cristina de Lena, south of Oviedo, on the way to León.

was built. What remains is impressive, with a series of intricately carved lattices, and some remaining fresco decoration. Carved panels appear to show gladiatorial or circus scenes. To get to Los Monumentos it's about a 30-minute brisk walk up Avenida de los Monumentos from above and behind the railway station. Bus No 3 plies the route hourly from Calle Uría, or it's a €5-7 cab ride from central Oviedo. From the bus, get off at the car park – Santa María is a five-minute walk up the hill; San Miguel a short way beyond. There's an Pre-Romanesque interpretation centre (free entry) on the road before you get to the monuments.

South from Oviedo → For listings, see pages 76-82.

Due south of Oviedo, just off the motorway to León, the town of **Mieres** can be accessed very easily on the **FEVE** *cercanías* from Oviedo (line F8). It's a likeably honest place, a working town which gives a taste of Asturian mining heritage. It has excellent nightlife, even more so during **Carnaval**, see page 81. Not far to the east, in the village of El Entrego, the **Museo de la Minería y de la Industria** ① *www.mumi.es, Oct-Jun Tue-Sat 1000-1400, 1600-1900, Sun 1000-1400; Jul-Sep Tue-Sat 1000-2000, Sun 1000-1400, €5*, is a proud display of the region's coalmining history. There is a good collection of working replicas of old mining devices, but the highlight is a guided descent into an excellent replica mine, bringing to life the conditions underground. El Entrego is accessed from Oviedo on a different *cercanía* line (hourly to El Entrego station on **RENFE** C2, and FEVE F6-F5 five times daily; get off at San Vicente if the train stops there).

Iglesia de Santa Cristina de Lena
① *Apr-Oct Tue-Sun 1100-1300, 1630-1830, Nov-Mar Tue-Sun 1100-1300, 1600-1800; €1.20. Contact the keyholder on T985 490 525 if there's no one about.*

South of El Entrego, overlooking the motorway near the border with León province, it's worth making the effort to visit another excellent pre-Romanesque church, Iglesia de Santa Cristina de Lena. Dating from the mid-ninth century, it's a pretty thing on the outside, but its hauntingly beautiful interior is better. A delicately carved raised triple arch is topped by symbols of early Christianity, not without some Islamic influence. The altar stone inscriptions have clear Visigothic/Germanic parallels, and there are several stones reused from a Visigothic edifice. To get there, take the *cercanía* line C1 to La Cobertoria, from where it's a short walk; thus avoiding the depressing town of Pola de Lena.

Parque Natural de Somiedo
Southwest of Oviedo, the national park (and UNESCO biosphere reserve) of Somiedo is a superbly high, wild area of Asturian forest, home to bears and wolves, as well as some exceedingly traditional Asturian villages. There are many superb walks in the park, one of the best starting from the hamlet of **Valle de Lago**, from where there's a walk to (you guessed it), Lago del Valle, a 12-km round trip up a high grassy valley with abundant birdlife. If you're see a dog the size of a pony, don't worry; these massive mastiffs are really big softies: unless you're a wolf. The trail is waymarked as PR 15.1. You can stay in Lago del Valle, or in the bigger village of **Pola de Somiedo**, a 1½-hour walk back on the main road.

West from Oviedo → *For listings, see pages 76-82.*

Salas
West of the fishing centre of Cornellana, along a valley of eucalyptus and wild deer, is the town of Salas, a small, picturesque, and tranquil place. Salas' most famous son was Hernando de Valdés, whose formidable presence still looms large in the town over 500 years after his birth. An extremely able theologian and orator, he rapidly ascended the church hierarchy until, in 1547, he became Inquisitor-General for the whole of Spain. His rule was, like the man himself, strict, austere and inflexible. Quick to crack down on any books, tracts or people with so much as a sniff of liberalism or reformation about them, he can be seen as a symbol of the Spain that turned its back on Europe.

Valdés came from a notable local family whose small castle and tower still dominate the town. Inside is the **tourist office** and a small **museum** ① *tourist office and museum, T985 830 988, turismo@ayto-salas.es; mid-Mar to mid-Jun and mid-Sep to Oct Tue, Thu-Sat 1000-1400, 1600-1830, Wed and Sun 1000-1400; Nov to mid-Mar Thu and Sat 1100-1400, 1600-1800, Sun 1100-1400, mid-Jun to mid-Sep Tue-Sun 1000-1400, 1700-2000; admission €1.20.* The museum, which is in the tower, has a display of pre-Romanesque inscriptions and ornamentation. The rest of the castle is mostly a hotel set around the pleasing courtyard.

Down the hill a little stands the **Colegiata de Santa María la Mayor**, where the body of the inquisitor now rests in an alabaster mausoleum.

Pravia and Santianes
Little-known **Pravia** is another small gem in the crown of Asturias. Founded in Roman times, it was briefly the home of the Asturian court in the eighth century before being forsaken for Oviedo in AD 808. Now a small agricultural town, its small centre is a relaxing collage of perfect façades, which are at their best in the soft evening light. The town feels oddly South American, perhaps as a result of the large numbers of *indianos* who returned home having made their fortunes in the new colonies. Many *indiano* houses dot Pravia and the surrounding area (as well as much of Asturias) – they are typically tall and grandiose,

and often have gardens planted with palms and cactus. In the heart of town there's a **tourist office** ① *Parque Sabino Moutas s/n, T985 821 204, Tue-Sat 1000-1300, 1600-1900 (1700-2000 summer), Sun 1030-1300.*

The centre of Pravia is presided over by the bulky **Colegiata de Pravia** and the connected **Palacio de los Moutas**, good examples of Spanish baroque architecture. The oldest building in the town proper is the **Casa del Busto**, a large and dignified *casona* now tastefully converted into a hotel. Built in the 16th century, it was a favourite refuge of Jovellanos, the 18th-century Spanish Enlightenment figure par excellence, whose sister-in-law lived here.

The nearby village of Santianes de Pravia, 3 km from town, has a church which is the oldest of the series of existing pre-Romanesque buildings of this size. It preserves little of its original character, having been substantially altered over the years, but is an attractive building nonetheless. It stands on the site of an earlier Visigothic church. Nearby, a **museum** ① *Tue-Sat 1030-1330, 1700-1900, Sun 1130-1330, €2*, displays finds from the recent restoration of the church, including a curious stone whose acrostic inscription makes it look like a word puzzle. The entry fee includes admission to the church, which is otherwise under lock and key.

Santianes is one stop from Pravia on the **FEVE** line and is also accessible by bus. To get there by car or on foot, go down Calle de la Industria from the centre of Pravia, cross the river and two roundabouts, and continue up the hill. Santianes is signposted to the right about 1.5 km up this road.

Oviedo and around listings

For sleeping and eating price codes and other relevant information, see pages 13-19.

🛏 Where to stay

Oviedo *p69, map p72*

There's a cluster of cheap accommodation near the train station on and around the main new town street C Uría.

€€€€ Hotel de la Reconquista, C Gil de Jaz 16, T985 241 100, www.hoteldela reconquista.com. Oviedo's top hotel is fantastically built around, and faithful to, the 18th-century Hospital of the Principality. Set around galleries, courtyards and chapels brimming with period objets d'art, the hotel makes up for in artistic charm what it lacks in top-of-the-range facilities. Visitors are welcome on the ground floor – it's well worth a look. Check the website for special offers.

€€€ Gran Hotel España, C Jovellanos 2, T985 220 596, www.granhotelespana.com. This noble giant is typical of a certain type of smart Spanish hotel slightly yearning

for the glory days of the 1920s. Untypically, this has been sensitively renovated, and the courteous staff complement the plush interiors. The rooms are equipped to business-hotel standard, and the location right on the edge of the old town is also a plus. Parking and Wi-Fi available.

€€€ Hotel Libretto, C Marqués de Santa Cruz 12, T985 202 004, www.librettohotel. com. Bright and vibrant, this strikingly innovative hotel faces the San Francisco park. Facilities are impressive, with DVD/ CD players, posh TV, rentable laptops, Wi-Fi access, and even an umbrella for the regular drizzle, but it's the sleek, opera-themed design that lives long in the memory. A minimalist mix of the classic and the avant-garde, it somehow works. There are often excellent weekend or promotional deals.

€€€ M Hotel, C Comandante Vallespín s/n, T985 274 060, www.mhotel.es. In a building created by Santiago Calatrava, this swish designer hotel certainly looks the part, and the interior decor lives up to it, with an eclectic mix of the modern and antique lending plenty of style and high degrees of comfort. Excellent facilities include a diner-style sushi bar; the only drawback is the less-than-central location.

€€ Hostal Arcos, C Magdalena 3, T985 214 773, www.hostal-arcos.com. A very friendly place in the heart of the old town, just off the Plaza de la Constitución. All rooms have small modern en suites; there's 24-hr access; basically it's a top central-city budget option. Recommended.

€€ Hostal Romero, C Uría 36, T985 227 591, www.hostalromero.net. Well located in the new town in shopping centre, this well-renovated *pensión* has big and inviting rooms, all with bathroom and TV. The owners are welcoming and enthusiastic. Recommended.

€€ Hotel Alteza, C Uría 25, T985 240 404. This is a decent, cheap hotel in a flamboyant building on Oviedo's main shopping street not too far from the station. The rooms are compact but snug, and there's a comfy guest lounge. All rooms have TV and bathroom; they are warm in winter and a little hot in summer. Breakfast included.

€€ Hotel Carreño, C Monte Gamonal 4A, T985 118 622, www.hotelcarreno.com. Handily located just behind the bus station, and in striking distance of the pre-Romanesque monuments, this hotel is run by nice people and features decent-sized rooms and modern bathrooms, all spotless. The price is more than fair, and a simple breakfast is included. Parking available. Recommended.

€€ Hotel Ciudad de Oviedo, C Gascona 21, T985 222 224, www.hotelciudadde oviedo.es. Right on cider street, this has unremarkable, but modern, spacious, spotless, and comfortable rooms. The free Wi-Fi works well and the staff are welcoming and helpful. It's much cheaper outside Jul-Aug.

€€ Hotel El Magistral, C Jovellanos 3, T985 215 116, www.elmagistral.com. The steel and bottle-glass decor gives an intriguingly space-age feel to this original establishment. The rooms are softer, well-lit and with lacquered floorboards and pastel colours accompanied by the expected facilities. It's well located, competently staffed and has parking available.

€€ Hotel Favila, C Uría 37, T985 253 877. Very handily placed for trains and buses and situated on Oviedo's main shopping street, this has comfy rooms with cable TV and smart bathroom, as well as cheery staff. The restaurant downstairs does a cheap, tasty and filling lunchtime *menú*.

€€ Hotel Fruela, C Fruela 3, T985 208 120, www.hotelfruela.com. An excellent location and helpful staff make this a wise choice. Smooth modern lines and shiny surfaces make it feel spotless, and everything seems to work the way it should. Prices vary wildly from **€€€€** to **€€** depending on availability – check online.

€€ Hotel Ovetense, C San Juan 6, T985 220 840, www.hotelovetense.com. In a prime central location just near Plaza Porlier, this hotel has cosy rooms, which, although small, are top value. It can be a little stuffy in summer, but it's quiet and friendly nonetheless. There's a restaurant and pay parking available nearby.

€€ Hotel Vetusta, C Covadonga 2, T985 222 229, www.hotelvetusta.com. This small and welcoming central hotel has modern design that exudes warmth and personality. All rooms are exterior – there's a little traffic noise but the light and life make up for it – and half come complete with a mini sauna/massage unit. There's a sunny café-bar downstairs. There's a parking station alongside and off-season rates are great. Recommended.

€ Hostal Belmonte, C Uría 31, T985 241 020, www.hostalbelmonte.com. An inviting and hospitable option in a lovely green and cream building, this is one of a range of budget accommodation on this street. It's been attractively renovated, with a wooden floor and a variety of rooms, all with TV and bathroom.

€ Pensión Fidalgo, C Jovellanos 5, T985 213 287. This homely, welcoming, and colourful set-up is well placed between the old and new towns and just a hop, skip and jump away from the cider houses of C Gascona. The rooms facing the street are a little noisy but the friendly old couple running it make up for it. Recommended.

Parque Natural de Somiedo *p75*
The best options to stay in the Somiedo area are the numerous excellent *casas rurales*. There are too many to deal with here; check www.toprural.com for a few enticing starting options.
€€ Meirel, T985 763 993. This appealing hotel in the centre of Pola de Somiedo is a good comfy spot to sleep and refuel on hearty Asturian food. Rooms are appealingly decorated in confident colours and rustic furnishings, and there are also apartments available.

Salas *p75*
€€ Castillo de Valdés-Salas, Plaza de la Campa s/n, T985 830 173, www.castillo valdesalas.com. This is an excellent rural hotel situated within the small castle, a beautiful setting indeed with its charming rustic central patio. The rooms are very true to the building but have much more than castle comfort. They feature bright homely fabrics on comfortable beds, pastel-shaded walls and polished floorboards. Recommended.
€ Hotel Soto, C Arzobispo Valdés 9, T985 830 037. This cheap hotel is set in a pleasant old building right next to the Colegiata, which the best rooms overlook. While far from luxurious, the rooms are heated and have bathroom and television, and the price is very reasonable.

Self-catering
The hills to the northeast of Salas have a number of good options for self-catering.
Ca Pilarona, Mallecina, T629 127 561, www.capilarona.com. One of the best options,

Ca Pilarona is in the tiny village of Mallecina, 11 km from Salas. It is a series of 5 restored houses, modernized with excellent facilities. They sleep from 2 to 6, and cost from €65-90 per night, depending on length of stay.

Pravia and Santianes *p75*
€€ Casona del Busto, Plaza Rey Don Silo 1, Pravia, T985 822 771, www.casonadel busto.es. One of the best places to stay in the area, this elegant hotel is set in a 16th-century *casona*. From the hallway to the rooms it's charming; the use of period-style furniture perfectly sets off an already striking building. The rooms all have individual character, with plenty of wooden furniture and hessian giving a taste of the colonial era. There's also a good restaurant, with tables in the open atrium. Recommended.
€ Pensión 14, C Jovellanos 8, Pravia, T985 821 148. This is a small and welcoming *pensión* with 2 home-from-home rooms, lavishly appointed with stove, sink, utensils, TV, pine wood and skylights. It's on a small street in the centre of town; don't confuse it with the hotel of the same name at the bottom of Pravia. Recommended.

🍴 Restaurants

Oviedo *p69, map p72*
Head to the 'Boulevard of Cider', C Gascona, for a wide choice of places to try the life-blood of Asturias; most also do tasty seafood.
€€€ Casa Conrado, C Argüelles 1, T985 223 919, www.casaconrado.com. Closed Sun and Aug. A fairly traditional Spanish *mesón*, all dark wood and cigar smoke, this is a local byword for quality and elegance. The cuisine has Asturian favourites accompanied by fine meat and fish dishes; main courses are €20-30 and there's a top wine list.
€€€ Casa Fermín, C San Francisco 8, T985 216 452, www.casafermin.com. Closed Sun. With a lovely atrium dining space adorned with ornate glassware, this central spot features really excellent service, a very fat wine list, and really tasty dishes ranging from

local specialities to more elaborate creations. Their *merluza a la sidra* (hake cooked in cider) an Asturian speciality. Recommended.

€€€ El Raitán, Plaza de Trascorrales 6, T985 214 218, www.elraitan.com. A long-term favourite for Asturian cuisine, this attractive establishment offers a smart, traditional restaurant alongside a typical Asturian cider bar. The restaurant mains are pricey but very tasty: this is an excellent place to try hearty dishes like *fabada* (bean and meat stew). There are various set menus at lunchtime (€20-40) including one for kids.

€€€ La Corrada del Obispo, C Canóniga 18, T985 220 048. This stylish restaurant on a lovely square near the cathedral is beautifully decorated, with plenty of natural light as well as chandeliers, polished wood floors and all the trimmings. The thoughtfully prepared food matches the surroundings and feels slightly underpriced. Delicious mains include such temptations as monkfish and sea bass in asparagus sauce. There's a €50 *menú de degustación* showcasing the best on offer. They also run the place next door, **Catu**, which focuses on tapas and seafood dishes.

€€ Bocamar, C Marqués de Pidal 20, T985 271 611, www.bocamar.es. In the heart of the shopping district, this is a warmly lit, reasonably upmarket fish and seafood restaurant that offers a good €18 *menú* at lunchtime.

€€ El Cachopito, C Gascona 4, T985 218 234. At the top of Gascona, this sets the tone with well-poured cider and a range of *cachopos*, a typical Asturian plate consisting of 2 thin fried breaded steaks sandwiching various combinations of fillings, costing from €14.

€€ El Cogollu, Plaza de Trascorrales 19, T985 223 983. This is a little gem of a restaurant in the southeastern corner of Plaza de Trascorrales. Its peaceful stone and ochre interior is decorated with traditional ceramics; there's imaginative freshly-prepared Asturian cuisine, including

delicious stews, great grilled vegetables, and tasty, fairly priced meat. Recommended.

€€ Faro Vidio, C Cimadevilla 19, T985 228 624. This extremely popular restaurant specializes in well-priced Asturian home cooking. The hearty stews and casseroles are simple and filling, while the extensive seafood dishes are prepared and presented in an uncomplicated and authentic manner.

€€ La Bellota Asturiana, C Fruela 16, T985 200 658. Popular for an after-work wine at 1400, the 'acorn' has a bar where they do a nice line in gourmet tapas and *montaditos* (little toasted sandwiches), while the pretty upstairs-downstairs dining areas offer elaborate and tasty plates as well as a *menú* that's a steal for around €10.

€€ La MásBARata, C Cimadevilla 2, T985 213 606, www.lamasbarata.com. A sparky modern but casual tapas bar specializing in rice dishes. It's popular with smart young Asturians who choose from a huge range of *raciones* for €6-13, delicious accompaniments to a *caña* at the bar; other mains are €9-19.

€€ Tierra Astur, C Gascona 1, T985 203 411, www.tierra-astur.com. Spacious and very popular, this cider house is one of the best-value places to eat in Oviedo. The solid wooden tables groan under the weight of some of the *raciones* that come out of the kitchen; many would feed 2, such as a selection of Asturian cheeses, all labelled with a cute little flag. The bar itself is convivial and has the smooth and lenient Trabanco cider. There's a lunchtime *menú* for €10.

€ Casa Montoto, C San Bernabé 9. This is a simple, no-frills establishment of a sort sadly dying out in Spain. The only adornment is photos of roller-hockey teams, but the crowds flock in for a cheap wine and a *bollo preñao*, a favourite Asturian snack consisting of chorizo sausage baked in a bread roll. They don't come better than they do here.

€ La Paloma, C Independencia 3, T985 235 397. An Oviedo classic, this double-sided bar swells with people for morning coffee or a pre-lunch vermouth and tapa, and it makes a good evening rendezvous-point. They have their own vermouth *solera,* which has been going over a century, there are daily specials such as paella, and smart seafood snacks; try some *bígaros* (winkles). They also do offer sit-down meals including a decent *fabada.*

€ **La Pumarada**, C Gascona 8, T985 200 279. A busy *sidrería* with impressively fast and efficient service. The excellent value *menú del día* offers a variety of Asturian and other specialities with wine for €10. The enormous portions may intimidate those on diets, but more robust diners will be able to savour cooking of a very high standard.

€ **Las Campanas de San Bernabé**, C San Bernabé 7, T985 224 931. An attractive faded façade in the shopping district conceals a popular restaurant with beautifully painted beams and a good line in bistro-style Asturian fare, seafood dishes and rices. It's deservedly busy, and has daily blackboard specials; the warming stews are particularly good, washed down with a jar of wine.

€ **Más Que Vinos**, Plaza Constitución 6, T607 823 404. In the heart of things, this modern bar has won a loyal local following for its upbeat and cordial atmosphere, delicious range of wines from around Spain, and free tapa with your drink. Folk congregate around the barrels outside on the square if the weather permits; if you can grab a table on the terrace, don't give it up lightly.

Cafés and bars

A traditional Oviedo pastry is the *carbayón,* an eclair-like almond creation. It's named after the oak tree, the traditional centre and meeting place of Asturian villages. A large *carbayón* was controversially chopped down in Oviedo in 1879 to make more room on C Uría; a plaque marks the spot where it stood.

Café Dólar, Plaza de Porlier 2, T985 215 876. An historic central café with a relaxed ambience and prime location. It's decorated with a modern but classical touch that seems somehow very characteristic of contemporary Oviedo.

Rialto, C San Francisco 12, T985 212 164. With over 80 years in business, the Rialto must be doing something right. Its pastries are widely considered the best in Asturias and are absolutely delicious; browse them at the counter at the front, then eat them at your leisure at the cosy tables in the rear.

South from Oviedo *p74*

Plaza San Juan in Mieres is an elegant little square easily recognizable by the statue of a cider-pourer in full flow. Its placement here is no accident, as several of the town's many excellent *sidrerías* are nearby.

€ **El Rinconín**, Plaza San Juan 5, Mieres, T985 462 601. One of the best of the *sidrerías,* and notably welcoming.

Salas *p75*

There aren't many places to eat in Salas.

€€ **Castillo**, Plaza de la Campa s/n, T985 830 175. Closed Tue nights. Undoubtedly the best option in town, this is the **Castillo de Valdés-Salas** hotel restaurant. It offers a cheap and tasty lunch *menú* and cooks up game, warming traditional plates, and some of the local trout catch in season. If you're not a guest and want dinner, phone ahead to reserve a spot.

€ **Bar La Campa**, Plaza de la Campa s/n, T985 832 220. A pleasing option for simple tapas and *raciones,* with a range of wines to accompany them. Its best feature is a breezy terrace over looking the castle.

Pravia and Santianes *p75*

€€€ **Balbona**, C Pico de Merás 2, Pravia, T985 821 162. Don't be fooled by the somewhat garish neon sign; this is actually a restaurant with a weighty reputation for quality Asturian fare. There's always a wide selection of fresh fish caught just down the road, while the beef is also recommendable. Despite the traditional atmosphere, there's plenty of modern flair in the preparation, as well as a bar where you can relax with tapas or a bottle of cider.

€ La Hilandera, C San Antonio 8, Pravia, T985 822 051. This good-looking *sidrería* is immediately recognizable by its green façade. There are various cheeses and meats to enjoy with the cider, as well as heartier *raciones* like tripe. Upstairs is a very cute stone-walled dining room, with a wider selection. *Raciones* are €5-8.

Bars and clubs

Oviedo *p69, map p72*
Many of the bars only open at the weekend. Much of Oviedo's nightlife is centred in the rectangle bounded by Calles Mon, Postigo Alto, San José and Canóniga. Other areas are C Rosal, for a grungier scene and, of course, the cidery area around C Gascona and C Jovellanos.

Ca Beleño, C Martínez Vigil 4. This is a legendary Oviedo bar focusing on the Asturian folk scene with its Celtic roots fully intact. They pour a great Guinness and the front garden is a fine place on a mild evening. Frequent live music. Check their Facebook page for concerts.

La Perrera, C Postigo Alto 5. This small, attractive bar is named 'the doghouse' and it's dedicated to rock 'n' roll from the 1960s on. Beware of the pooch signs in various languages that provide the decor.

Swing Jazz Club, C Cañóniga 14. Around the side of the cathedral, this new café bar is deservedly popular for its inclusive atmosphere and live music at weekends. Check its myspace page, www.myspace.com/swingjazzclub, for upcoming concerts.

Entertainment

Oviedo *p69, map p72*
Cinema
The **Cajastur** bank on Plaza de la Escandalera has a programme of art house films.

Theatre
Teatro Campoamor, Plaza del Carbayón, T985 207 590, www.teatrocampoamor.es.

A well-regarded mainstream theatre programme, opera performances, and weekly Sun morning concerts of Asturian folk music.

Festivals

.Oviedo *p69, map p72*
Feb/Mar   Carnaval in Oviedo is a big affair; the main day here is the Sat after **Shrove Tue**, ie 43 days before **Easter Sun**,when you can see the traditional end of Carnaval ceremony: the burial of the Sardine.
Sep   Oviedo's major festival is the fiesta of **San Mateo**, the city's patron. The 3rd week of Sep is given over to street parades, dances, bullfights, an opera season and other celebration.

Shopping

Oviedo *p69, map p72*
Oviedo is a good place to shop, with a wide range of chain and boutique outlets. C Uría is the place to find smart fashion, as are the pedestrianized streets east of it.

Books
La Palma Libros, C Rúa 6, T985 214 782. Good bookshop for information on Asturias; also has a good English-language section.
Librería Cervantes, C Doctor Casal and C Campoamor. Bookshop with an excellent range of English-language books, as well as Asturian and Spanish literature.

Department stores
El Corte Inglés, C Uría 9. A **Corte Inglés** superstore with anything you could want.

Food
Mercado El Fontán, behind the Plaza Mayor. This covered central market is a good place to stock up on Asturian produce. The curious might be interested in the horse butcher.

⊖ Transport

Oviedo *p69, map p72*
Air

Flights arrive into and depart from Asturias international airport, see page 69. Buses run hourly (on the hour) from Oviedo's bus station to the airport, taking 45 mins and costing €6.35. A taxi costs about €50.

Bicycle hire

Salvador Bermúdez, C Postigo Alto 1, T985 212 326, rents and repairs bicycles.

Bus

Local city buses are blue and run on 13 clearly marked routes around the city (see www.tua.es for a map). The basic fare is €0.90. Bus No 3 runs hourly from C Uría up to Santa María de Naranco and San Miguel de Lillo. The intercity bus terminal is near the train station (T902 499 949, www.estaciondeautobusesdeoviedo.com). There are many buses to **Gijón**, 30 mins, and many companies run services across Asturias. The major intercity operator is ALSA (www.alsa.es), T902 422 242, who connect **Oviedo** with **A Coruña** (3 daily, 4-6 hrs, €22), **Santiago** (3 daily, 5-7 hrs, €27), **León** (9 daily, 1½ hrs, €9), **Valladolid** (5 daily, 4 hrs, €19), **Madrid** (14 daily, 5½ hrs, €32), **Santander** (10 daily, 2½-3½ hrs, €14), and **Bilbao** (9 daily, 5 hrs, €21). Some of these services are premium class, meaning they're slightly quicker and more expensive.

Taxi

Call T985 220 919 if you can't flag one on the street.

Train

There is a bewildering number of short-distance *cercanía* train routes around the central valleys of Asturias. These are run by both FEVE and RENFE out of the train station. Details of individual lines can be found in the relevant destination section.

For long-distance services, RENFE links Oviedo with **Madrid** (4 daily, €50, 4¾ hrs) via **León** (6 daily, 1¾ hrs, €20) and **Valladolid** and with **Barcelona** (2 per day, 11 hrs, €52), and points in between. FEVE's coastal network links Oviedo (slowly) with **Santander** (2 through trains per day, 4 hrs, €15), **Bilbao** (1 per day, 6½ hrs, €23), and westwards as far as **Ferrol** in Galicia (2 per day, 6½ hrs, €22).

South from Oviedo *p74*
Mieres

Train FEVE trains run to Mieres from **Oviedo** (Line F8, frequent, 20 mins), and most southbound RENFE trains also stop here.
Bus There are regular buses from **Oviedo** and **Gijón** (at least hourly, 35 mins).

Parque Natural de Somiedo *p75*

Bus ALSA runs 4 buses on weekdays and 1 on weekends (leaves at 1000) to **Pola de Somiedo** (2 hrs 15 mins).

Salas *p75*

Bus ALSA runs hourly buses to/from **Oviedo**, 1 hr 15 mins, via **Cornellana**.

Pravia and Santianes *p75*

Train Pravia is served hourly by FEVE trains from **Oviedo** (Line F7) and **Gijón** (F4), 1 hr.

Bus ALSA also runs buses here to/from Gijón every couple of hours and takes 1 hr.

❶ Directory

Oviedo *p69, map p72*
Language schools Alea, C Fray Ceferino 10, T985 216 349, www.mund oalea.com. A highly professional company that organizes Spanish courses in Oviedo. Good reputation. **Medical services** There's a large **medical centre** that deals with emergencies at C Naranjo de Bulnes behind the train station, T985 286 000.

Gijón and Avilés

Following what seems to be the established law for such things, there is no love lost between Gijón and Oviedo. People in Gijón, the larger of the two, feel that it should be capital of Asturias instead of Oviedo, which some consider posh, soft and effete. Those in Oviedo aren't too bothered, but occasionally enjoy riling Gijón by referring to it, tongue in cheek, as 'our port'.

Gijón is a fun city picturesquely set around two sandy beaches and a harbour. The larger and nicer of the beaches, Playa de San Lorenzo, is an Asturian Copacabana, fronting 2 km of city blocks with a stretch of very clean sand, which almost wholly disappears at high tide – and in summer, under rows of bronzing bodies. There are a few decent waves to surf and a good-time feel in the warm months. The small old quarter, at the base of the Cimadevilla promontory, is heady with the yeasty cider smell from dozens of small bars. The council has also done a good job of highlighting the city's heritage with small museums and information plaques. In the local dialect, Bable, Gijón is written and pronounced 'Xixón'.

A little further west is Avilés, whose reputation is slowly changing. For a long time, the only travellers to pass through this large industrial centre were business visitors under company orders. Now, having tackled its pollution problems, the city is capitalizing on its major asset, a remarkably beautiful historic centre. On the back of its carnival, widely regarded as the best in Northern Spain, Avilés makes a concerted effort to welcome tourists. While there aren't many bona fide sights to visit, the beauty of the centre, the quality of the cafés and restaurants, and the openness of the people make it an excellent destination. Moreover, the beach is within walking distance, and it's a handy 10 minutes from Asturias airport.

Arriving in Gijón

Getting there Gijón is under 30 minutes' drive from Oviedo by motorway. The bus station is on Calle Magnus Blikstad, with regular long-distance connections to other cities in Northern Spain and local regional services. Just about all buses inbound from and outbound to other provinces stop in both Oviedo and Gijón. Train services depart from the nearby **FEVE** station on Plaza del Humedal. Most **RENFE** trains stop here too, although the main RENFE station (Gijón Jovellanos) is on Avenida de Juan Carlos I, about 20 minutes' walk from the old centre. ▸▸ *See Transport, page 91.*

Tourist information The helpful **municipal tourist office** ① *Dársena Fomento pier, T985 341 771, www.gijon.info, daily 0900-2000 (2200 in summer)*, is just around the harbour from the old town. The staff are multilingual and well informed. There's also a network of summer information kiosks, including one at each end of San Lorenzo beach.

Sights

The Ayuntamiento of Gijón has been busily populating the city with small museums of varying degrees of interest. See www.gijon.info for a full list of them. There are also numerous small art exhibitions leading brief lives in unlikely places. At the tip of the Cimadevilla headland is a small hill, the **Cerro Santa Catalina**, which is topped by the remains of a castle and crowned by Eduardo Chillida's *Elogio del Horizonte*, a giant concrete sculpture that has become the symbol of the town. If you stand beneath it, you can hear the sound of the waves below. Below the hill stands the equally photographed *Nordeste*, a work by Joaquín Vaquero Turcios.

A few blocks back through the old town's web, the birthplace of Jovellanos has been turned into the **Museo Casa Natal de Jovellanos** ① *Plaza Jovellanos, T985 185 152, Tue-Fri 0930-1400, 1700-1930, Sat-Sun 1000-1400, 1700-1930, free*. It's basically Gijón's art gallery; more interesting than the handful of Jovellanos memorabilia are the modern works of Navascués and the massive wooden depiction of the old Gijón fish market by Sebastián Miranda, a work he patiently restarted from scratch after the first was lost during the Civil War.

Although now a bank, the succinctly named, sandstone **Palacio del Marqués de San Esteban del Mar de Natahoyo** is one of Gijón's most beautiful buildings, particularly in the evening sun. Behind it, the **Plaza Mayor** leads a double life as stately municipal square and lively hub of cider drinking.

The **Playa de San Lorenzo** stretches to the east of here, watched over by the **Iglesia de San Pedro** and a statue of Augustus Caesar, who stands near the entrance to the city's moderately interesting remains of the Roman public baths, **Termas Romanas** ① *T985 185 151, Tue-Fri 0930-1400, 1700-1930, Sat-Sun 1000-1400, 1700-1930, €2.40, free Sun*. The beach's long boulevard is the natural choice for an evening *paseo*.

At the other end of the beach, the sluggish **Río Piles** is flanked by pleasant parks studded with palms. On the east side, about a 10-minute walk back from the beach, is the **Museo del Pueblo de Asturias** (Muséu del Pueblu d'Asturies) an open-air ethnographic park with reconstructions of various examples of traditional Asturian buildings and life. Also in the complex is the **Museo de la Gaita** ① *both Paseo del Doctor Fleming s/n, T985 182 963, Oct-Mar Tue-Fri 0930-1830, Sat-Sun 1000-1830. Apr-Sep Tue-Fri 1000-1900, Sat-Sun 1030-1900; €2.40, free on Sun*, devoted to bagpipes from around the world. Bagpipes have a long history in Asturias – the local type has a more austere tone than the Scottish kind. Information (audio)

Gijón

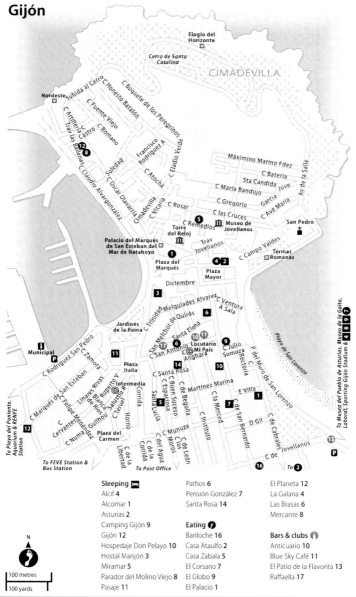

Sleeping 🛏
Alcif **4**
Alcomar **1**
Asturias **2**
Camping Gijón **9**
Gijón **12**
Hospedaje Don Pelayo **10**
Hostal Manjón **3**
Miramar **5**
Parador del Molino Viejo **8**
Pasaje **11**
Pathos **6**
Pensión González **7**
Santa Rosa **14**

Eating 🍴
Bariloche **16**
Casa Ataulfo **2**
Casa Zabala **5**
El Corsario **7**
El Globo **9**
El Palacio **1**
El Planeta **12**
La Galana **4**
Las Brasas **6**
Mercante **8**

Bars & clubs 🍸
Anticuario **10**
Blue Sky Café **11**
El Patio de la Flavorita **13**
Raffaella **17**

is Spanish only. The museum has a *sidrería*/restaurant with a pleasant terrace. On the other side of the river, by the **Sporting Gijón** stadium, is the busy Sunday *rastro* (flea market).

Beyond here, about 3 km from the centre, is the massive and curious structure of the **Universidad Laboral**, whose pitiless bulk evokes the Franco years; it's usually considered the nation's largest building. Begun as a project to help children who had lost their fathers to mining accidents, it soon became a larger affair dedicated to teaching traditional trades. Part of the space has recently been given over to form **Laboral** ① *T985 185 577, www. laboralcentrodearte.org, Wed-Mon 1200-2000, €5, free Wed,* an excellent and enthusiastic museum of contemporary art and design. The vast and interesting spaces of the former workshops are put to good use, with concurrent temporary exhibitions of high quality. They also have concerts, theatre performances, and other cultural events. It's easily reached by bus (Nos 1, 2, 4, or 18) from the centre of Gijón.

Gijón's other beach, **Playa de Poniente**, is a short walk west of the centre. It's also nicely sanded, but has more industrialized views. At its western end is the **Gijón Aquarium** ① *Sep-Jun Mon-Fri 1000-1900, Sat and Sun 1000-2000, Jul-Aug daily 1000-2200, €12, €6 for children.*

Around Gijón
Northwest of Gijón, the seaside towns of Candás and Luanco sit on the headland of Cabo Peñas, which ends in the cape of the same name, where an exhibition in the lighthouse explains something about the sealife of the area and the history of the building itself. Candás and Luanco make relaxed, family-friendly places to stay, close to the sights of Gijón but quieter.

Avilés and around → *For listings, see pages 87-91. Phone code: 985. Population: 84,242.*

The heart of Avilés is **Plaza de España**, from which a number of scenic pedestrian streets radiate. One side of it is occupied by the **Ayuntamiento**, an attractive arched building that is a symbol of the post-medieval expansion of the town. Opposite is the elegant bulk of the **Palacio del Marqués de Ferrera**, now converted to a luxury hotel. Avilés' **tourist office** ① *C Ruiz Gómez 21, T985 544 325, turismo@ayto-aviles.es, Mon-Fri 0900-1400, 1630-1830, Sat and Sun 1000-1400, daily 1000-2000 in summer, very helpful, English spoken,* is a block down from Plaza de España. From the Plaza de España (many locals refer to it as the Plaza Mayor), Calle San Francisco runs up to the **Plaza Domingo A Acebal**, where it becomes the colonnaded Calle Galiana. This area is lined with bars and cafés, several of which have tables outdoors. It's a popular and recommended evening meeting spot. Calle San Francisco is dominated by the 13th-century **Iglesia de San Nicolás de Bari** with a pretty Romanesque cloister, now partly occupied by a school. In front is the **Fuente de los Caños** (fountain of the spouts), which pours water into a basin from six lugubrious faces. Further up Calle Galiana, the **Parque de Ferrera** was part of the impressive back garden of the counts of Ferrera before being given over to public use. It's now a rambling network of paths.

On the other side of Plaza de España, Calle Ferrería leads into the oldest part of town; this part of the city was originally walled. At the bottom of the street are the early Gothic **Capilla de los Alas**, and the earlier **Iglesia de los Padres Franciscanos**, started in the late 12th century. The latter's sandy Romanesque façade is appealing; inside is the tomb of a notable *avilesino*, Pedro Menéndez, who founded the city of San Agustín in Florida (which claims to be the oldest city in the USA). West of here, in the **Plaza Camposagrado**, is a statue of another famous local, the shaggy Juan Carreño de Miranda, a notable 17th-century Spanish painter. A few blocks further west again, past the waterfront park of **El Muelle**, is Avilés' prettiest square, the **Plaza del Carbayo**. This is in the barrio of **Sabugo**, where the majority of Avilés fisherfolk used to live. It was almost a separate town, and the plaza was its centre, where whaling and fishing expeditions were planned. Walking back towards town along Calle Bances Candamo gives further flavour of this tiny district. Between Sabugo and the centre, Plaza Hermanos Orbón, which holds the market, is memorable for its high arcade and windowed balconies glinting with dozens of panes of glass.

The nearby town of **Salinas** (4 km northwest of Avilés) is a somewhat bland place whose raison d'être is its long, sandy beach, thronged in summer but quiet at other times. At its western end is one of Asturias' best restaurants, **Real Balneario**, see page 90, and a the view from the headland is good; there's also a vaguely surreal collection of anchors. Salinas can be reached by city buses Nos 1 and 11 from Avilés bus station.

Gijón and Aviles listings

For sleeping and eating price codes and other relevant information, see pages 13-19.

⊖ Listings

Gijón *p84, map p85*
Gijón bristles with hotels, but many are dull cells for business travellers. Happily, there are several options with more charm.
€€€ Hotel Alcif, Camino de los Quiñones 513, T984 117 700, www.hotelalcif.com. Perfect for those who like a quiet urban base, this new hotel is situated in a residential complex not far from the campsite in the eastern end of town. It's extremely peaceful, beautifully decorated, has a great garden and is run in a most welcoming manner. It's **€€** off-season. Recommended.
€€€ Hotel Alcomar, C Cabrales 24, T985 357 011, www.hotelalcomar.com. Although slightly starchy, this hotel has an excellent location at the old-town end of the San Lorenzo beach. The rooms with a view (some €20 more) are predictably lovely and light, and come with minibar, safe and the standard conveniences of a hotel of this level. There can be some noise from late-night revellers though. Breakfast included.
€€€ Hotel Pasaje, Marqués de San Esteban 3, T985 342 400, www.hotel pasaje.net. With views of the marina from some of the rooms, this hotel makes the most of its central, but tucked-away location. The rooms are comfortable,

with decent Wi-Fi access and modern bathrooms. It's overpriced in Jul and Aug, but a great deal (**€€**) the rest of the year.
€€€ Hotel Pathos, C Santa Elena 6, T985 176 400, www.celuisma.com. This is a refreshingly offbeat modern crash pad close to the Plaza Mayor and beach. Pop art decorates the walls and each of the small but stylish rooms is dedicated to a 20th-century icon: Jagger? Thatcher? Gandhi? Your choice. Bathrooms are modern and swish, while there's Wi-Fi, minibar, and a safe in the rooms. Great value off-season.
€€€ Hotel Santa Rosa, C Santa Rosa 4, T985 091 919, www.bluehoteles.es. Decked out in minimalist white with the odd blue object as a feature, this chic recently opened hotel offers plenty of comfort and modern facilities on a central pedestrian street. Appealing and stylish without being in the least pretentious.
€€€ Parador del Molino Viejo, Av Torcuato Fernández Miranda s/n, T985 370 511, www.parador.es. This parador, in a suburban setting in a duck-filled park at the eastern end of Gijón, is mostly modern but its restaurant is set within the walls of an old mill. Rooms are spacious, stylish and well lit. It's a little hard to find; look next door to the riverside **Sporting Gijón** football stadium.
€€ Hotel Asturias, Plaza Mayor 11, T985 350 600, www.hotelasturiasgijon.com. There's little luxury or boutique enchantment at this spot, but it's got the

best location of any Gijón hotel, right on the Plaza Mayor, steps away from restaurants, harbour, cider bars, and the beach. It's a simple establishment, with fair prices, rooms with enough light and space, and an OK included breakfast. Staff are friendly.

€€ Hotel Gijón, C Pedro Duro 6, T985 356 036, www.hotelgijon.com. Readers put us on to this good-value hotel a short walk from the train and bus stations and not too far from the Plaza Mayor. Spacious rooms are a steal off-season and the staff are helpful and keen to please. They also have apartment-style rooms available.

€€ Hotel Miramar, C Santa Lucia 9, T985 351 008, www.hotelmiramargijon.com. Although right in the heart of Gijón's shopping and bar-hopping area, this small hotel is remarkably quiet. The friendly management keep the rooms just-so. Can get stuffy in summer.

€€ Hospedaje Don Pelayo, C San Bernardo 22, T985 344 450, www.hostal donpelayo.com. This upmarket *hostal* is in a noble old townhouse very close to the beach. The rooms are comfortable and bright, with gleaming modern bathrooms, heating, hairdryers and cable TV. Much cheaper off season.

€ Hostal Manjón, Plaza del Marqués 1, T985 352 378. Very well-located *hostal* just a few paces from the restaurant and cider action of the Plaza Mayor. Rooms with a view are much nicer but noisier. The furniture and fittings are old, and don't expect extras like TV or Wi-Fi, but it's a reliable budget spot.

€ Pensión González, C San Bernardo 30, T985 355 863. Basic but wholesome option with high ceilings, wooden floorboards, and a significant population of porcelain dogs. Bathrooms are shared but ok. Particularly cheap off-season.

Camping

Camping Deva, 4 km east of town just off the highway, T985 133 848, www.camping deva-gijon.com. Well-equipped campsite

with a swimming pool, and lines of simple cabins and better-equipped bungalows. Gets busy in summer.

Camping Gijón, T985 365 755, www. camping-gijon.com. Well situated at the tip of the headland to the east of the Playa de Lorenzo.

Around Gijón *p86*

€€ Hotel Plaza, Plaza de la Baragaña 6, Luanco, T985 880 879, www.laplazahotel. net. In the centre of Luanco near the beach, this chic but welcoming hotel has attractive modern rooms, some of which are larger than others. There's a decent variety of breakfast options too. Cheaper off season.

Avilés and around *p86*

€€€ Palacio de Ferrera, Plaza de España 9, T985 129 080, www.nh-hotels.com. This hotel has been sensitively converted from a 17th-century palace right on the main square in the heart of Avilés. The rooms aren't cheap, but they have all the facilities of a business hotel, room service, gym, sauna, and underground parking. Rates vary extensively depending on availability and the time of year. Extras like internet access are overpriced.

€€ Hotel Don Pedro, C La Fruta 22, T985 512 288, www.hdonpedro.com. Just down the hill from Plaza de España, this small hotel is run out of a busy café. The staff are welcoming, the stone-faced rooms are charmingly grotto-like and have an Arabian feel. Recommended.

€ Hotel de la Villa, Plaza Domingo A Acebal 4, T985 129 704, sebucansl@ telecable.es. This likeable hotel is well situated in the historic centre, looking over a pleasant plaza and the church of San Nicolás de Bari. Rooms are appealing, with dark wood floors and prints of Kandinsky and Klee, and the staff are friendly.

€ Pensión La Fruta, C La Fruta 21, T985 512 288. This well-equipped *pensión* is run out of the friendly **Hotel Don Pedro**, and is directly opposite it. Every room comes with its own bathroom (either en suite or next to the room), and TV. Recommended.

🅟 Restaurants

Gijón *p84, map p85*

Gijón offers some excellent eating around the Plaza Mayor and the marina. The black spiny *ericios* (sea-urchins) are a local favourite, as are *zamburiñas* (a tasty small scallop). Near the Plaza Mayor, C Salustio Regueral is a destination for smart tapas bars specializing in wine rather than cider. At the far end of the San Lorenzo beach (turn left to hug the headland) are several good options with magnificent views of the sea and sand. The pricey Bellavista is the classiest, and the cheap and cheerful Las Terrazas del Pery the most popular.

€€€ Casa Ataulfo, C Cabrales 29, T985 340 787. This *sidrería* is one of Gijón's most reliable for excellent fresh seafood. Ask what's good that day: they take the finest fish from the market, and things like calamari or *berberechos* (cockles) are always brilliant. Recommended.

€€€ Casa Zabala, C Vizconde de Campo Grande 2, T985 341 731, www.casazabala. com. Near the Jovellanos museum, this Cimadevilla restaurant is run by a family, now in its 4th generation, who show a sure touch in dealing with fruits of the Bay of Biscay as well as dishes more rooted in the traditions of the Asturian farmland. The dining room is *acogedor* – a Spanish word that is somewhere between comfortable and welcoming.

€€ El Corsario, C Marqués de Urquijo 16, T985 338 620. It's worth tracking down this small local just back from the southeastern end of the San Lorenzo beach for its warm service and excellent-value meals. Try the *brocheta de secreto ibérico* – 2 skewers of succulent acorn-eating pork that melts in the mouth.

€€ El Globo, C San Bernardo 13, T985 172 247, www.sidreriaelglobo.es. There's more elbow-room in the downstairs dining area than the stuffy upstairs one at this excellent traditional cider house. Great *bígaros* (winkles) and whole baked calamari (*de potera*) can be accompanied by an excellent cheeseboard featuring Asturian products. Recommended.

€€ El Palacio, Plaza de Marqués 3, T985 341 368. Closed Mon. In an elegant restored building between the port and the Plaza Mayor, with a popular cider joint and terrace downstairs. Above is quite an elegant restaurant. Some tables have fine views over the harbour. The *magret de pato* (duck magret) is delicious, as is the seafood and salads.

€€ El Planeta, Tránsito de las Ballenas 4, T985 350 056, www.el-planeta.net. It doesn't look like much when you walk in, but this no-frills place by the leisure harbour is an excellent choice for cider and seafood. A typical Gijón place and one of the most popular, so be prepared to wait for a table: they don't take bookings. Specialities are calamari and, in summer, *ventresca de bonito* – tender meat from around the belly area of the bonito fish.

€€ La Galana, Plaza Mayor 10, T985 172 429. This distinguished looking *sidrería* on the main square is a prime spot to eat and drink, and a good introduction to Asturian cider culture, with understanding bar staff who pour well and look after you. The huge barrels, painted ceiling and heavy wooden beams give plenty of atmosphere. You can snack on tapas (€3-5 for a decent plate), or head up the back for some more serious seafood and stews. The lunchtime *menú* is great value at €11 for 4 courses.

€€ Mercante, Cuesta del Cholo 2, T985 350 244. A very good harbourside option with an excellent €10 lunch *menú* in the upstairs restaurant. In fine weather, a popular choice is to grab a cold drink from the bar and sit on the stone wall outside. Recommended.

€ Las Brasas, C Instituto 10, T985 356 331. No-frills *parrilla* restaurant with a range of *platos combinados* and *menús*. Things such as *chorizo criollo* (an Argentinian sausage) are particularly tempting. The half *parrilla* €16; €20 with salad) can comfortably feed 2 people and features a range of meats. Eat upstairs for a quieter meal.

Cafés

Bariloche, Plaza del Instituto 1, T985 350 169. One of the city's classic cafés, with a characteristic duplex style in vogue in the 1970s in Spain. There are tasty rolls and good coffee; a good breakfast. Free Wi-Fi.

Around Gijón *p86*
€€ **Sidrería El Muelle**, Paseo del Muelle s/n, T985 880 035. In the most appealing part of Luanco by the harbour, this is an old local favourite with a great outdoor terrace. The seafood *raciones* are well prepared and fairly priced. Go for mussels, grilled bonito, sardines (*parrochas*) or fresh grilled calamari. Recommended.

Avilés and around *p86*
Avilés is an excellent place for eating out; especially C Galiana and the old streets north of Plaza de España.
€€€ **Real Balneario**, Av Juan Sitges 3, Salinas, T985 518 613, www.restaurante balneario. com. One of Asturias's top restaurants, beautifully set on the beach at Salinas. Specializing in seafood, the €24 lunch *menú* is definitely the most economical way to enjoy the haute cuisine, but you might be tempted by the multi-course degustation or 'gourmet' set meals. Presentation is exquisite, and the wine list most extensive.
€€ **Casa Lin**, Av de los Telares 3, T985 564 827. This is a historic *sidrería* near the station serving up excellent seafood and well-poured cider. *Fabada* and kidneys stewed in sherry (*riñones al jerez*) also are reliably good.
€€ **Casa Moisés**, C La Muralla 4, T985 526 000, www.casamoises.com. For casual cidery dining, head to this spacious and popular offering, with a boisterous atmosphere and simple plates of high-quality food, especially fish and seafood.

Prawns, *cigalas*, sea urchins: it's all good here. The *menú* for €9 is also great value.
€€ **Casa Tataguyo**, Plaza del Carbayedo 6, T985 564 815, www.tataguyo.com. Tough to find with its small sign, this wonderful split-personality restaurant has been an legend for years. The traditional bar dishes out cheap workers' lunches at shared tables in a satisfyingly no-frills atmosphere, while up the back you can dine on very classy Asturian fare in a comfortably cordial setting.
€€ **La Posada**, C Ruiz Gómez 12, T985 510 117. This restaurant is across the road from the tourist office and is warmly decorated in a modern but traditional style on 2 levels. There are plenty of warming Asturian stew-type dishes, and they prepare fine *bacalao* (cod). There's a lunch *menú* for €13 midweek, and other set meal options at various prices.
€€ **Llamber**, C Galiana 30, T984 832 348. Tucked away under the stone colonnade of this attractive street, this top-quality new restaurant offers modern Spanish cuisine drawing on influences and ingredients from around the nation. Tuck into dishes like peach and quail salad on the burner-warmed barrel terrace.

Cafés

Café Don Pedro (see Where to stay). Set in the hotel of the same name, this café is decorated in similar stony style. The coffee is very good.
Cafetería El Piano, C Alfonso VII 3, T985 512 333. Cosy and friendly, this is a place to seek out a morning coffee, which will come accompanied by a tasty small cake or slice of tortilla.

Bars and clubs

Gijón *p84, map p85*
There are many cheerful drinking bars along C Rivero off the Plaza de España. The small streets around C Santa Lucía are a mass of bars, many operating only at weekends.
Anticuario, C San Antonio 9, T985 344 441. A fairly upmarket café during the day, this

place changes once the sun goes down, as a white-collar (and mixed) crowd move from the *café con leche* to the gin and tonics. Particularly lively at weekends; closes late.

Blue Sky Café, C San Antonio 6, T985 356 141, next door to **Anticuario**. This compact place is a reliable option; dark, sleek, styled. A DJ and lively crowd turns it into a disco at weekends.

Raffaella, C Santa Elena 21, T699 139 085. This cheery Italian-run cocktail bar with cute lighting, cosy white vinyl seating, and outrageously colourful drinks is a winner.

El Patio de la Favorita, C Ezcurdia 5. A fine spot for an evening drink, this moodily-lit place is on the beachfront, very spacious, and features regular live music. In summer there's a gimmicky camera so you can keep an eye on the beachfront action.

Avilés and around *p86*
The main area for weekend nights is the barrio of Sabugo, where pubs around C Estación are always busy. The no-frills bodegas along C Rivero also fill up fast.

✪ Festivals

Avilés and around *p86*
Feb/Mar Carnival, known as *Antroxu*, in Avilés is big. The town happily submits to a week of parties and events centred around the Plaza de España. On the Sat, C Galiana sees a riotous procession of boats on a river of foam, while the Tue hosts a more traditional, but equally boisterous, procession. The whole town is in fancy dress, including the bars, which also undergo a change of identity. **Ash Wednesday** sees the traditional **Burial of the Sardine**. Accommodation is tight, but **FEVE** run trains all night from Gijón and Oviedo on the main nights.

⊖ Transport

Gijón *p84, map p85*
Air Flights from Asturias international airport, see page 69, reached by bus from Gijón hourly on the hour, 40 mins, €6.35. A taxi is €45.

Bus Local services run regularly to **Oviedo** (30 mins) and **Avilés** (30-40 mins). The major intercity operator is ALSA, www.alsa. es, T902 422 242, who connect Gijón with **A Coruña** (4 daily, 5-6 hrs, €25), **Santiago** (4 daily, 6 hrs, €29), **León** (9 daily, 2 hrs, €12), **Valladolid** (5 daily, 4½ hrs, €21), **Madrid** (14 daily, 6 hrs, €35), **Santander** (10 daily, 3-4 hrs, €16), and **Bilbao** (9 daily, 4 hrs, €23). Some of these services are premium, being quicker and more expensive.

Ferry A new ferry service between Gijón and **St Nazaire** has started to operate as a trial at time of research. Run by GLD Atlantique, www.gldatlantique.co.uk, the overnight crossing takes 14 hrs. Foot passengers are not accepted; you must have a vehicle and take a cabin.

Train FEVE coastal connections to **Santander** (2 daily, 4 hrs, €15), **Bilbao** (1 daily, 6½ hrs, €23), and westwards as far as **Ferrol** in Galicia (2 daily, 6½ hrs, €22). More regular services run to **Llanes**, **Cudillero** and **Avilés**.

RENFE links Gijón with **León** (7 daily, 2½ hrs, €22), **Madrid** (4 daily, 5¼ hrs, €51), **Barcelona** (2 daily, 11-13 hrs, €52-71) and points in between.

Avilés and around *p86*
Air Flights from Asturias international airport, see page 69, reached by regular bus, 25 mins, €1.35. A cab to the airport costs about €22.

Bus and train The RENFE, FEVE, and bus stations are on Av de los Telares on the waterfront to the west of the old town. Both **RENFE** and **FEVE** connect the town frequently with **Oviedo** and **Gijón** (35-40 mins), as does the bus company ALSA. Frequent buses for western Asturias.

Western Asturias

The west coast of Asturias is a rugged green landscape, speckled with fishing villages and gouged by deep ravines. George Borrow describes the arduousness of crossing these in the 1830s in The Bible in Spain, but nowadays they are spanned by massive road and rail viaducts. It makes a great place for an enjoyably low-key Asturian stay. The fishing towns of Cudillero, Luarca and Tapia de Casariego bristle with character, and there are many excellent beaches, some with good surf.

Southwestern Asturias is something of a wilderness, whose steep green valleys still contain villages that are not accessible by road. It's a hillwalker's paradise: there are several good bases with a range of marked trails, such as Santa Eulalia de Oscos, or Taramundi, famous for its knives and centre of a fascinating ethnographic project. The village of Grandas de Salime is another rewarding place to stay and is home to an excellent ethnographic museum. It's also worth applying to visit the Parque Nacional Muniellos, in the far southwest corner of Asturias – the old-growth European forest is home to several endangered species, including a small community of bears.

West coast → *For listings, see pages 96-101.*

Arriving on the west coast

The A8 motorway runs west just back from the coast, and is being completed in stages, while the **FEVE** line from Gijón and Oviedo to Galicia also follows this coast faithfully, although the stations tend to be at a short distance from the town centres, and there are only three trains a day in either direction. **ALSA** buses are much more frequent.
▸▸ *See Transport, page 101.*

Cudillero and around

The colourful houses of this small fishing town are steeply arrayed around the harbour like the audience in a small theatre. Its picturesque setting and small fishing harbour make this prime outing territory during summer holidays. Entirely dormant during winter, in season Cudillero makes a good destination, having enough restaurants and bars to keep things interesting, but still not suffering from resort-style over-development. It's a lovely place.

The town, called *Cuideiru* in Bable, effectively has just one street, which winds its way from the village of El Pito, replete with *indiano* mansions, down the hill into Cudillero and down to the harbour, which is the easiest place to park. Here, the new **tourist office** ① *Puerto del Oeste s/n, T985 591 377, turismo@cudillero.org; Jul-Sep daily 1000-2100, Oct and Apr-Jun Mon-*

El Cambaral

El Cambaral was the most famous of the Moorish pirates who terrorized the Cantabrian and Asturian coasts. The scourge of local shipping, he was finally tricked by a local knight, who put to sea in an apparently harmless ship that was actually bristling with hidden soldiers. El Cambaral was wounded and captured. The knight took him home, for the trial had to wait until the accused had healed, but foolishly his captor let his young daughter tend to the pirate's wounds.

The two predictably fell in love and decided to elope. Reaching the port, where a boat was waiting, and thinking themselves safe, they stopped for a kiss, but the enraged knight had been warned. He arrived at the quay and chopped off both the kissers' heads with one blow.

Luarca remembers the ill-fated couple in the name of its bridge, *El Beso* (The Kiss), and the fishermen's quarter, known as *El Pirata Cambaral*.

Fri 1000-1400, 1700-2000, Sat 1100-1400, 1700-2000, Sun 1100-1400; Nov-Mar Mon-Fri 1000-1400, 1600-1900, Sat 1100-1400, 1600-1900, Sun 1100-1400, can furnish you with information on the town; apart from a small exhibition (€1) in the former *lonja*, there's not a lot to see; the setting and atmosphere is the main attraction. Most of the action takes place around the waterfront, where the smell of grilling fish is all-pervading at lunchtime.

There are some wildly shaped cliffs in this area, and while the summer sea might seem almost Mediterranean, in winter the waves give the sea wall a pounding. **El Pito**, just off the main road east of town, has its own **FEVE** station and a few places to stay. It's an attractive walk down into the town but an uphill return trip.

Luarca

The charm of Luarca, one of this coast's best destinations, is that although summer visitors are drawn by its attractive harbour and plentiful facilities, it gives the refreshing impression that fishing remains its primary concern. While it has grown a little since Borrow exclaimed that it "stands in a deep hollow ... it is impossible to descry the town until you stand just above it", it's still a compact place, centred around the Río Negro, a stream in summer that swells substantially in colder months. Luarca was formerly a major whaling port; the whale still has a proud place on the coat of arms.

Once again, the **harbour** is the biggest attraction, filled with colourful boats of all sizes. A variety of restaurants line it; beyond them you can walk around to the sea wall and watch it take a fearful pounding if the sea is in the mood. At the other end of the harbour is the **beach**, a rather apologetic affair with dirty grey sand and lined with changing huts. A much better beach is **Playa de Taurán**, a few kilometres further west.

Just by the water opposite the church is the *lonja*, where the freshly caught fish is sold throughout the day. It's decorated with tiled murals depicting the town's fishing history, one of which shows the curious custom of deciding whether to put to sea or not in bad weather: a model of a house and of a boat were put at opposite ends of a table and the fishermen lined up according to their preference. If the majority chose to stay home, nobody would go to sea that day. The **tourist office** ① *C Los Caleros 11, T985 640 083, turismo@ayto-valdes.net, Tue-Sat 1000-1400, 1630-1830, to 2000 in summer and Sun 1100-1400, 1700-1900*, is by the river at the western end of town.

Navia and around

At the mouth of the river of the same name, Navia is a more commercial port than the others on this coast, with a significant boat building and plastics industry. Unlike most of the others, Navia's charm is to be found away from its harbour, in the narrow paved streets of the old town above. The **tourist office** ① *top of C Las Armas, T985 473 795, turismo@ayto-navia.es; Oct-Jun Thu-Fri 1030-1330, 1600-1800, Sat 1030-1400, 1600-1830, Sun 1030-1330; Jul-Sep Tue-Fri 0930-2100, Sat and Sun 1000-1400, 1600-1930*, is in this part of Navia.

There's plenty to do around Navia. From town you can walk 10 km east along a marked coastal trail, rewarded by magnificent views and a good dollop of sea air and pine resin in your lungs.

The valley of the Río Navia, winding inland to **Grandas de Salime** and beyond, is one of Asturias' natural highlights, dotted with Celtic *castros*, small hillforts, most of which are between 2000 to 2500 years old. While some of the remoter ones are well worth exploring with transport, the most accessible is just 6 km from Navia, at **Coaña** ① *T985 978 401; Oct-Mar Tue-Sun 1030-1500; Apr-Sep Tue-Sun 1030-1400, 1600-1900, closed Mon; free*. A series of circular house foundations are compactly arrayed within a walled precinct on the hillside, commanding a spur in the valley and guarded by a tower that would have been the only entry point to the community. There are free hourly guided visits in the summer months. There's a café and a small visitor centre. Infrequent buses run there from Navia; if you want to walk, cross the bridge over the river and take the first road on the left. The fort is a short way past the village of Coaña.

Tapia de Casariego and around

Tapia, one of the most relaxed places on this coast, deserves a look. While there is a small harbour, the town's beautiful beach west of the centre is deservedly the main attraction. There's a small surf community here, established by the semi-mythical Gooley brothers – two Aussies who fetched up in a campervan one day in the 1970s – and it certainly feels more like a beach town than a fishing port. The town itself is charming, with a quiet elegance radiating from its whitewashed stone buildings and peaceful plazas watched over by the dominant Christ on the church tower. Opposite the church, there's a small tourist information kiosk open in summer. Apart from Tapia, the best surf beaches are **Peñarronda** to the west, where there are two campsites, and **Frejulfe**, further east. Waves also get ridden under the bridge that crosses into Galicia between Castropol and Ribadeo to the west.

Castropol and the Galician border

Asturias ends at the Ría de Ribadeo, a broad estuary at the mouth of the Río Eo, notable for the cultivation of shellfish. The N634 highway blazes straight on over a massive bridge into Galicia. While the main town in this area, Ribadeo, is across the water, Asturias still has a little more to offer in the village of Castropol.

With a great setting on the estuary, the village is a peaceful and seldom-visited gem. Formerly an important ferry crossing, it has been completely bypassed by the massive bridge, and now does little but cater to passing traffic on the Lugo road. If you've got a spare hour or two, it won't be wasted exploring the narrow streets of this lovely place. The central plaza contains a memorial to the Spanish-American war of 1898. The naval defeats of this war, and subsequent decline in shipping due to the loss of all Spain's remaining colonies, were big factors in the decline of towns on this coastline. To reach Castropol, take the Lugo turn-off from the coast road a few kilometres before Galicia.

Southwest Asturias → *For listings, see pages 96-101.*

Arriving in southwest Asturias
Travelling is time-consuming on these remote roads, even with your own car.
➡ *See Transport, page 100, for details of buses.*

Taramundi and around
More easily accessed from the coast, the road to Taramundi beetles up green valleys where mules and donkeys still draw carts, and herds of cows take priority over vehicles. The village itself is an earthy place, which draws its fair share of summer tourists, many of whom are attracted by its numerous knife workshops. The Taramundi blades are renowned throughout Spain; the range available runs from professional-standard kitchen knives to carved tourist souvenirs. Most of the workshops welcome visitors – there are plenty to choose from. Taramundi is only a couple of kilometres from Galicia, and the locals speak a bewildering mixture of Bable and Galego that they cheerfully admit is incomprehensible to outsiders. There's a **tourist office** ① *Av Solleiro 18, T985 646 877, Tue-Sun 1000-1400, 1630-1930*, on the main road at the bottom of town.

In the valley around Taramundi are a number of ethnographic projects, where traditional Asturian crafts and industries have been re-established. The best of these is possibly **Os Teixois** ① *T985 979 684, www.osteixois.com, daily 1100-1800, €1.50, free Wed*, in an idyllic wooded valley with a working mill and forge powered by the stream. If there aren't many people about, it feels uncannily as if you've just stepped back in time. There's a small restaurant, which cheerfully serves up simple but abundant food, much of it produced by the local projects. Teixois is about one hour's walk from Taramundi – head straight down the hill and follow the signs. The road passes near several of the other projects en route.

Grandas de Salime
This sleepy little municipal centre is notable for an excellent museum, the **Museo Etnográfico** ① *Sep-Jun Tue-Sat 1130-1400, 1600-1830, Sun 1130-1430, Jul-Aug Tue-Sun 1130-1400, 1600-1930, €1.50*, an ambitious and enthusiastic project that seeks to recreate in one place a range of traditional Asturian crafts, industries and daily life. Working mills, grape presses, and pedal-operated lathes are fascinatingly and lovingly put to work by the informative staff. Here you can see the making of the characteristic *madreñas*, wooden clogs worn over shoes when working outdoors, still very much in use. It's an important project and indicative of the deep pride Asturians hold for their heritage.

Reserva Natural Integral de Muniellos
① *Access is strictly limited to 20 visitors a day; reservations are taken on T985 105 545.*
This large protected area of mountain oak forest is situated west of the AS-15 some 30 km south of Cangas. Much of it is unspoiled old-growth forest and it is home to many protected species including badgers, capercaillie, deer, bears, short-toed eagles, otters and serpents. The enthusiastic visitor centre is 7 km from the main road and is the starting point for a seven-hour walking trail through the forest. One inhabited village remains in the far north of the park. These days you can count the inhabitants on the fingers of one hand, a sad example of the depopulation of the Asturian mountains.

Western Asturias listings

*For sleeping and eating price codes and other
relevant information, see pages 13-19.*

● Where to stay

Cudillero and around *p92*

€€ La Casona de la Paca, El Pito, T985
591 303, www.casonadelapaca.com.
Closed Jan. This red 3-storey house is
a typical *casa de indiano* with a walled
garden. Fairly formal in style, it's a relaxing
and secluded hideaway. As well as the
comfortable rooms, there are also good-
value apartments for daily or weekly hire.
Take the 1st (ie easternmost) turn-off for
Cudillero, and you'll see it on your right.
It's just 5 mins' walk from the El Pito train
station (turn left out of it).

€€ La Casona del Pío, C Riofrío 3,
Cudillero, T985 591 512, www.lacasona
depio.com. Closed Jan. This beautiful stone
hotel and restaurant is just off the harbour.
It's run by warm and friendly people, and
has welcoming compact rooms with
hydromassage mini-tubs. The food is great.
Recommended.

€€-€ Pensión El Camarote, C García
de la Concha 4, Cudillero, T985 591 202,
www.elcamarote.es. In the top half of
the main street, this upmarket *pensión*
has well-equipped rooms but is often full
in summer, so book ahead. They give a
substantial discount to pilgrims walking
to Santiago. Light breakfast included.

€ Pensión Alver, C García de la Concha 8,
Cudillero, T985 591 528, www.pensionalver.
com. Open Easter-Sep. On the main street
through the village, this friendly *pensión* in
a bright blue building has good-standard
rooms that are as clean as a whistle. There's
free internet and Wi-Fi, and use of a kitchen.

Camping

Camping Cudillero, T985 590 663,
www.campingcudillero.com. Open
May-Sep. Some distance east of the town,

but appealing and friendly, offering good
facilities including cabins. Handy for the
El Aguilar beach.

Luarca *p93*

€€ Hotel Báltico, Paseo del Muelle 1, T985
640 991, www.hotelbaltico.com. Right on
the harbourside, this solid family-run hotel
offers a great position and quiet rooms
with plenty of light. There's a new annexe
with more upscale modern rooms, some of
which have great views over the port.

€€ Hotel Rico, Plaza Alfonso X, 6, T985
470 585, www.hotelrico.com. An excellent
budget option, this has value-packed
and spacious rooms above a café. There's
cable television, heating and good en
suite bathrooms. Heated debates from
downstairs can echo through the building,
but it's a winner at this price and a steal
off-season. Recommended.

€€ Hotel Villa de Luarca, C Alvaro de
Albornoz 6, T985 470 703, www.hotelvilla
deluarca.com. Occupying a characterful
centenarian mansion in the heart of town,
this worthwhile spot features individually
decorated rooms with furniture befitting
the building and plenty of pleasing small
features. The boss can tell you about the
best beaches and hidden spots in the area.
This price only applies in late Jul and Aug;
the rest of the year it's cheaper.

€€ La Colmena, C Uría 2, T985 640 278,
www.lacolmena.com. This attractively
modern option has smallish but newly
refurbished rooms with attractive wooden
floors and furnishings and plenty of light.

€€ Torre de Villademoros, T985 645 264,
www.torrevillademoros.com. Between
Cudillero and Luarca, this is a beautiful old
Asturian farmhouse with an extremely
stylish modern interior situated on a
cliff above the sea with a large medieval
tower in its backyard. The rooms are most
commodious, and the friendly owners
have just created a romantic and luxurious

suite in the tower itself – perfect for an upmarket family break, or a romantic getaway. Delicious home-made food is a highlight. From Villademoros on the main road (buses stop here), cross the railway bridge and turn left when you reach a small *parrillada*. The hotel is signposted from there. Recommended.

€ Pensión Moderna, C Crucero 2, T985 640 057. A simple, old-style *pensión* with 3 spotless doubles and polished floors.

Camping
Playa del Tauran, T985 641 272, www.campingtauran.com. Open Easter-Sep. The best campsite in this part of Asturias, on a clifftop west of Luarca with access to a small beach. Excellent atmosphere and facilities. Bar, shop and cabins are among the eucalypts. It is 3 km from the main road, near the hamlet of San Martín. Quicker access by foot from the far end of Luarca beach. Recommended.

Navia and around *p94*
€€€ Hacienda Llamabúa, La Mabona, T985 474 981, www.haciendallamabua. es. Between Luarca and Navia, this modern rural hotel is good for a families, with plenty of grounds to wander, a pool and child-friendly facilities. The rooms are comfortable, decorated contemporary-rustic with up-to-date conveniences like plasma screen TVs and iPod docks. They also have self-catering apartments available.

€€ Hotel Arco Navia, C San Francisco 2, Navia, T985 473 495, informacion@ hotelelarco.com. Attractive slate building by an arch on a historic medieval street. Apparently St Francis stayed in what is now the rental apartments.

€€ Hotel Casona Naviega, Av Emigrantes 37, T985 474 880, www.casonanaviega.com. This winningly blue *indiano* house sits on the main entrance road to Navia and offers a pleasing combination of original features and modern conveniences like Wi-Fi and a DVD library. It's run by enthusiastic young owners and surrounded by a pleasant garden featuring the palm trees so characteristic of these buildings. The rooms are compact but attractively furnished.

€€ Hotel Palacio Arias, Av Emigrantes 11, Navia, T985 473 671, www.palacioarias. es. One of the most lavish and eccentric *indiano* constructions in western Asturias, surrounded by a walled garden and furnished in period style. Go for the superior rooms in the *palacio* itself; the hotel's modern annexe is cheaper but less characterful.

€ Pensión San Franciso, C San Francisco s/n, Navia, T985 631 351. On a tiny plaza, this whitewashed *pensión* is clean and simple.

Tapia de Casariego and around *p94*
Accommodation in Tapia is unremarkable but adequate.

€€ Hotel Puente de los Santos, Av Primo de Rivera 31, T985 628 155, www.hotelpuentedelossantos.com. On the main road, where the buses stop. The rooms are a little bit old fashioned, but comfortable enough for a beach break for a couple of days.

€€ La Xungueira, T985 628 213. Closed Oct-Mar. By the beach, on the main road just west of the centre, this is the best option in Tapia. The pastel-shaded rooms are comfortable if not particularly inspiring; some of the bigger ones have fold-out couches. There's also a cider bar and a big garden with playground to keep the kids onside. Significant off-season discounts.

Camping
Camping Playa de Tapia, T985 472 721. On the other side of the beach from town, this summer-only campsite has reasonable facilities. Road access a couple of kilometres west of town but on foot it's much quicker across the beach.

Castropol and the Galician border
p94

€€€ Palacete de Peñalba, C El Cotarelo s/n, Figueras, T985 636 125, www.hotel palacetepenalba.com. On the hill above Figueras, this flamboyant apricot-coloured edifice dominates the fishing village. Set in a huge garden, it was built in the early 20th century by a modernista disciple of Gaudí. It's now a lavish place with an expensive French-influenced restaurant.

€€ Peña Mar, Ctra General s/n, T985 635 482, www.complejopenamar.com. The nicer of the 2 uninspiring hotel-motel set-ups on the main road.

Taramundi and around *p95*

€€€ La Rectoral, Cuesta de la Rectoral s/n, Taramundi, T985 646 760, www.la rectoral.com. This historic hotel is housed in the 18th-century building that used to be the home of the parish priest, with superb views over a fairytale valley. The rooms are extremely comfortable – the best have balconies overlooking the valley, as does the dining room.

€€ Casa Petronila, C Mayor s/n, Taramundi, T985 646 874, www.casa petronila.com. Attractive rooms in an old stone building on the main street.

€€ Hotel Taramundi, C Mayor s/n, Taramundi, T985 646 727, www.hotel taramundi.com. This friendly hotel has bedrooms plumb-full of Asturian comfort. It's a small and intimate place and real care has been paid to the decoration. Recommended.

€ Pensión La Esquina, C Mayor s/n, T985 646 736. The cheapest beds in town in a simple *pensión* above a café. Small and comfy (unless you're tall, as the beds have footboards).

Casas de aldea

The area around Taramundi is brimming with *casas de aldea*. 2 recommendable ones are **€€-€ Freixe**, T985 621 215, near the village of Barcia, and **€ Aniceto**, T985 646

853, www.casavillar.com, a small nucleus of houses in Bres. Pricier, but with character and setting is **€€ As Veigas**, T987 540 593, www.asveigas.com, where, as part of the ethnographic project, a deserted village has been restored to life; the 2 buildings of the priest's house can be rented.

Reserva Natural Integral de Muniellos *p95*

The nearest accommodation to the park is on the main road.

€ Hotel La Pista, T985 911 004, www.hotel lapista.net. A short distance south of the turn-off, in the village of Vega de Rengos, dominated by a massive coal plant. It is welcoming, however, with colourful rooms, a restaurant and a cosy sitting room.

€ Pensión La Pescal, T985 918 903, www.lapescal.com. In the tiny village of the same name north of the turn-off, this is more a hotel than a *pensión*, with a garden, elegantly quirky bedrooms with the original furniture of the old house and comforting home-cooked meals. Great value.

🍴 Restaurants

Cudillero and around *p92*

There are plenty of seafood 'n' cider places of varying quality, many featuring meet-your-meal-style aquarium tanks.

€€ El Faro, Río Frío 4, T985 900 092. Perhaps the pick of the litter, tucked away just off the square at the bottom of town, this warmly lit and decorated seafood spot serves enormous portions in a cordial manner. Try the Asturian classic *merluza a la sidra* (hake cooked in cider), preceded by a shared plate of steamed *berberechos* (cockles) or anything else that takes your fancy. Recommended.

€€ La Casona del Pío, see Sleeping, above. An excellent seafood restaurant in the slate dining room with layered wooden ceiling. The philosophy is to produce '*cocina de siempre*' with high-quality ingredients; they succeed. Lunch *menú* for €20.

€€ Restaurante Isabel, C La Ribera 1, T985 590 211. Bang on the harbour with lifebuoy-and-anchor style nautical decor and appropriately high-class seafood.

€ Bar Julio, Plaza La Marina s/n, T985 590 124. A good café. Sitting on the outside terrace between the *soportales* you can watch on the whole town stretching up above you. They do decent bar-top munchies like *empanada* and little sandwiches.

€ El Ancla, C Riofrío 2, T985 590 023. Seafood restaurant specializing in paella and a mixed seafood *parillada*, but also does a range of *raciones* and tapas. The calamari are particularly tasty, generous portions.

Luarca *p93*

€€€ Restaurante Sport, C Rivero 8, T985 641 078. This smart harbourside joint specializes in seafood and especially shellfish, including river oysters from the nearby Río Eo. It is characterized by excellent service and a great wine list, whose various delights are served in lovely large glasses. There's also a bar, where they'll try and tempt you to dine by serving a delicious free *tapa*.

€€€ Villa Blanca, Av de Galicia 25, T985 641 035. Another gourmet option in town, with a choice of dining rooms. The seafood is of excellent quality, as you would expect from this proud fishing town, paintings of which decorate the walls.

€€ El Barómetro, Paseo de la Muelle 4, T985 470 662. The old wooden object in question stands on the wall outside this excellent seafood restaurant. The decor is warmly maritime, and the host is solicitous. Try a whole oven-baked *sargo* (white sea bream) or the *oricios* (sea urchins), which have an unusual but acquirable taste. High-quality dining at a very reasonable price. Recommended.

€€ Mesón de la Mar, Paseo de la Muelle 35, T985 640 994. Massive old stone building on the harbour with plenty of character and a big range of *menús*. There are also tasty *raciones* to be eaten at homely wooden tables in the bar, which features a circular table and trough for pouring your own cider. They also do excellent seafood rices for 2 (€30-40).

€€ Miramar, Paseo de Muelle 33, T985 640 584. On the top of the old *lonja* at one end of the harbour, this tempts with outdoor dining and drinks on a deck offering stunning views over the town and the port. The seafood has such offerings as *zamburiñas* (little scallops) or octopus straight off the grill at pretty reasonable prices.

€ Café Riesgo, C Uría 6, T985 640 818. Overlooking what passes for the town's traffic hub, this is a pleasant 1st-floor café with lots of windows for contemplation.

€ Cambaral, C Rivero 14, T985 640 983. Named after the swashbuckling pirate, see page 93, this is a great tapas and drinks option. There's a conservatory space with directors' chairs for a quiet coffee, while the bar is always lively with locals. The tapas are simple but delicious, like mussels or *lacón*.

Navia and around *p94*

€€€ La Barcarola, C Las Armas 15, T985 474 528. Fairly upmarket restaurant in a heavy 3-storey stone building in the old part of town. Attractive interior with dark wood and soft, coloured lights. Good reputation in these parts, particularly for seafood rice.

€€ El Sotanillo, C Mariano Luiña 24, T985 630 263. Restaurant with a range of seafood with a good *menú del día*. Café upstairs does a range of snacks for smaller appetites.

Tapia de Casariego and around *p94*

The majority of restaurants and bars are huddled around the harbour. Fresh fish is understandably their stock-in-trade.

€€ El Bote, C Marqués de Casariego 30, T985 628 282. This thoughtful seafood restaurant has a very homely feel and excellent fresh fish. Try the *percebes* (goose barnacles) if they are on offer.

€ La Cubierta, C Travesía del Dr Enrique Iglesias Alvarez, T985 471 016. A good *sidrería* with a simple and effective layout. A long bar crowded with locals is faced by wooden tables on 1 side, which need to be sturdy in order to support the massive *raciones* on offer at knock-down prices.

Castropol and the Galician border *p94*
€€ El Risón, El Puerto s/n, T985 635 065. Closed Feb. The best option in town for a meal or a drink, this is a friendly and peaceful place on the water with outdoor tables looking over the oyster and clam beds of the *ría*, and over to Ribadeo in Galicia.

Taramundi and around *p95*
All 3 Taramundi hotels have good restaurants.
€€ Hotel Taramundi, C Mayor s/n, Taramundi, T985 646 727. In the centre of town, and attractively stone-faced. The meat dishes stand out; the *churrasco* (ribs) and *solomillo* steak are particularly juicy.
€ Pantaramundi, C Mayor s/n, T985 646 821. Their bread is prized throughout Asturias. A friendly café, good for snacks.
€ Sidrería Solleiro, T985 646 706, further down the hill. A cheerily decent cider bar serving uncomplicated and delicious traditional fare.

① Bars and clubs

Luarca *p93*
Saint Michel, C Párroco Camino 28, T985 640 289. The liveliest of Luarca's bars, this long dark nightspot on the pedestrian main street gets lively at weekends, when it's open very late.

Navia and around *p404*
El Bar de Siñe, C Las Armas 17, Navia. A good bar on one of Navia's nicest streets.
Te Beo, Av del Muelle. One of Navia's best bars, with a good range of beers.

Tapia de Casariego and around *p94*
El Faro, El Puerto 10. By the harbour, this is a friendly bar decorated with photos and paintings of lighthouses. A good place to discuss the surfing options hereabouts.

❹ What to do

Luarca *p93*
Jatay, based 3 km west of Luarca, T985 640 433/600 665 763, www.jatayaventura.com. Organizes tours on horses and quad buggies in the area; on more of a holiday-fun than serious-trekking footing.
Valdés Aventura, T689 148 295. Offers more serious adventures on mountain bikes or on horseback.

Castropol and the Galician border *p94*
Ondabrava, based near Castropol, T985 627 341, www.ondabrava.com. Organizes an excellent range of activities throughout the region.

⊖ Transport

West coast *p92*
Bus ALSA buses run westwards more or less hourly along the coast from **Gijón** and **Oviedo** (changing at Avilés).

Cudillero and around *p92*
Bus Most ALSA services only stop on the main road about 30 mins' walk away. A few go into town; these mostly go to/from **Avilés**.

Train The railway station is at the top of the town.

Luarca *p93*
Bus The bus station is next to **El Arbol** supermarket on Paseo de Gómez on the river. There are regular bus services to/from **Oviedo**, **Gijón** and **Avilés**.

Train The FEVE station is a little further upstream, on the accurately named Av de la Estación, 10 mins' walk from the centre of town.

Navia and around *p94*
Bus The ALSA station is on the main road, Av de los Emigrantes. **Autos Piñeiro** service the Navia valley to **Grandas de Salime**.

Train The FEVE station is on Av Manuel Suárez, Navia. There are 3 services a day to and from **Oviedo** (2 of which continue to **Galicia**).

Tapia de Casariego and around *p94*
Bus ALSA buses stop on Av Primo de Rivera in the centre of town.

Train The FEVE station is an inconvenient 20-min walk.

Taramundi and around *p95*
Bus The closest bus stop to Taramundi is Vegadeo, 18 km away on the N640 that links Lugo with the Asturian coast.

Grandas de Salime *p95*
Bus A daily bus runs to/from **Oviedo** to Grandas de Salime, stopping at every house on the way. It takes 4 hrs and costs €13.

East coast Asturias

The coast east of Gijón is popular with Spanish summer tourists but it's always possible to get away from the crowds; the sheer number of small villages and accommodation options sees to that. The scenery is majestic, with rolling green farmland, little fishing communities tumbling down to the sea and, muscling right up to the coast, the spectacular Picos de Europa mountain range. There are also dinosaur footprints scattered around; pick up the tourist office brochure or hit the museum at Lastres if you're interested in tracking them down. You'll find some good examples, although not to the standard of those in the Rioja.

Villaviciosa and around → *For listings, see pages 104-108.*

Set back from the sea on a marshy inlet, Villaviciosa is a busy market town with an attractive historic centre. It's famous for *avellanas* (hazelnuts), but more importantly, it's the foremost producer of cider in Asturias, and is worth a visit even if you don't fancy trying the local juice. **Tourist office** ① *Plaza Obdulio Fernández 51, T985 891 759, www. lacomarcadelasidra.com, Oct-Mar 1200-1400, 1530-1730, Apr-Sep 1000-1400, 1600-1900.*

The centre boasts several elegant *indiano* buildings, as well as a church, the **Iglesia de Santa María de la Oliva** ① *Tue-Sun 1100-1400, 1700-1900*, a Romanesque building with very attractive zigzagged portals.

In a square nearby is a statue of Carlos V (Carlos I of Spain). In 1517, intending to make his first entry to Spain a grand one, Carlos' fleet was ravaged by storms and finally managed to limp into harbour at Tazones just north of here, thus making Villaviciosa his first sizeable stop. He stayed at a nearby *palacio*, **Casa de Hevia** ① *C José Caveda y Nava*, which is marked with a plaque.

A good chunk of the town's population work in the **cider factories**, some of which are open for tours, such as **El Gaitero**, a 10-minute walk from the centre. The tourist office will give details of visiting hours for this and others.

North of Villaviciosa, at the western mouth of its *ría* (estuary), the village of Tazones, where Carlos V washed up, is a picturesque place brimful of seafood restaurants. It gets busy with day trippers at weekends, gorging themselves on enormous rice-with-lobster dishes and suchlike. If it's the beach you want though, head up the eastern side of the estuary to Rodiles.

Southwest of Villaviciosa at a distance of about 10 km is the ninth-century pre-Romanesque **Iglesia de San Salvador de Valdediós** ① *T985 892 324, Nov-Apr Tue-Sun 1100-1300, May-Oct Tue-Sun 1100-1300, 1630-1800, €1*, one of the province's finest. Believed to have been the spiritual centre of the Asturian kingdom and part of a palace complex for Alfonso III, it is attractively proportioned with its typical three naves and carved windows. Plenty of paintwork remains, as well as charming leafy capitals and dedicatory inscriptions. Bat-phobes should avoid the place; several of the little creatures call the dark church home.

Lastres and around → *For listings, see pages 104-108.*

Lastres is a quiet and appealing fishing port with attractive views over the sea and rocky coast. Its steep streets see plenty of summer action, but little at other times, when the town gets on with harvesting *almejas* (clams) and fishing. The town makes a good, relaxing waterside stay, even when the nights are chillier and the sea mist rolls over the green hills.

MUJA ① *Rasa de San Telmo s/n, T902 306 600, late Sep-late Jun Wed-Sun 1030-1430, 1600-1900, late Jun-late Sep daily 1030-1430, 1600-2000, adult/child €6.60/4.40*, is the Jurassic Museum of Asturias and sits 1.5 km east of Lastres off the Colunga road. Built in the form of a dino's footprint, it serves as an interpretation centre for the area, which is rich in fossilized pawprints. Reconstructed skeletons as well as fibreglass models bring the giant creatures to life. Some 3 km away by road, **Playa La Griega**, is an excellent beach shaped strangely by a small river. There are sets of dinosaur prints on the southeast side, and a decent campsite, **Costa Verde**, see page 104.

Ribadesella → *For listings, see pages 104-108.*

Ribadesella is a town of two halves, separated by a long bridge. On the western side is the beach, a long, narrow strip of sand with plenty of accommodation and holiday homes behind it. Across the bridge is the fishing port, a more characterful area with plenty of good eating and drinking options, particularly in the summer season. The **tourist office** ① *Paseo Princesa Letizia s/n, T985 860 038, oficinaturismo@ayto-ribadesella.es, Oct-Jun Mon-Sat 1000-1400, 1700-2000, Sun 1100-1400, Jul-Sep daily 1000-2200*, is near the bridge on the harbourside. They have a leaflet of suggested themed circular walks from town, ranging from two to five hours in duration.

Just outside the town is a good place for a break from the beach, the **Cuevas Tito Bustillo** ① *Apr-Aug Wed-Sun 1000-1630, visits (1 hr) every 25 mins, €2.40, not recommended for children under 11*, a limestone cave complex with some prehistoric art from the Magdalenian culture that created Altamira, only discovered in 1968. Groups of up to 25 people are admitted every 25 minutes, but there's a daily limit, so get there earlier rather than later in summer. There's a small information hall and another cave alongside, open all year, which offers geological formations but no rock art.

The Sella river that flows into the sea here is a popular venue for canoeing, see page 107 for details of tour operators. The riotous descent of the Sella from Arriondas in August culminates here in one of Northern Spain's biggest parties.

Llanes → *For listings, see pages 104-108.*

Llanes is the most important town on this stretch of coast and a delightful place to stay. Although it sees plenty of tourists, it has retained a very pleasant character around its fishing port and walled, pedestrianized medieval centre. There are plenty of good beaches within reasonably easy reach. It was an important whaling town, and still hauls in a good quantity of smaller sea creatures every day; the best spot to see them is in the *lonja* where they are sold off daily at around midday. The **tourist office** ① *C Alfonso IX s/n, T985 400 164, www.llanes.com, turismo@ayuntamientodellanes.com, Mon-Sat 1000-1400, 1600-1830 (1700-2100 summer), Sun 1000-1400*, is located in an old tower within the walled town.

There's a tiny beach close to the town walls, **Playa del Sablón**, which soon fills up in summer. For more breathing room, head 20 minutes' walk east to **Playa de Toró**.

At the end of the harbour wall, Basque artist Agustín Ibarrola had the idea of cheering things up by painting the concrete blocks in exuberant colours. The *Cubes of Memory* are striking and best viewed from near the lighthouse on the eastern side of the harbour.

Towards Cantabria → *For listings, see pages 104-108.*

The last stretch of Asturias has many beaches and pretty pastures, with looming mountains in the background. Just across in Cantabria, **Devatur** (see What to do, page 107) run all kinds of canoeing, rafting and horse-riding activities.

East coast Asturias listings

For sleeping and eating price codes and other relevant information, see pages 13-19.

● Where to stay

Villaviciosa and around *p102*
€€ Casa España, Plaza Carlos I 3, Villaviciosa, T985 892 030, www.hcasa espana.com. This friendly and attractively renovated *indiano*-style house offers a cordial welcome in the café downstairs, and spacious bedrooms with comfort if little luxury, antique features like gnarled wooden headboards but plenty of modernity in their gleaming bathrooms. It's a steal off season but not the warmest (**€**).

Lastres and around *p103*
€€€€ Palacio de Luces, Ctra AS-257 s/n, T985 850 080, www.palaciodeluces. com. 2 km inland from Lastres, this 5-star complex is a recent conversion of an historic *palacio*. Rural in feel but luxurious in every particular, it makes a relaxing stop. The spacious rooms feature excellent bathrooms, and huge windows throughout the building offer great views of the Picos. Staff are solicitous and attentive. Prices are high but there's a restaurant, Wi-Fi, and numerous other thoughtful details.
€€ Hotel Eutimio, C San Antonio s/n, Lastres, T985 850 012, www.casaeutimio. com. At the switchback where the road to the port meets the main road winding down through the town, is this well-maintained

and modernized old *casona* with friendly staff and good seafood restaurant.

Camping
Costa Verde, T985 856 373. This grassy beachside campsite is open Jun-Sep.

Ribadesella *p103*
There are many places to stay; both in the centre, and along the beach, where there's a series of desirable hotels in converted *indiano* mansions.
€€€€ Villa Rosario, C Dionisio Ruiz Sánchez 6, T985 860 090, www.hotel villarosario.com. As striking as any of the *indiano* buildings along this coast, this ornate blue mansion has a prime beachside position and good rooms with top views and a restaurant. It's difficult to say it offers value in high summer, but it's a better **€€€-€€** outside of Jul-Aug.
€€€ Hotel Ribadesella Playa, C Ricardo Cangas 3, T985 860 715, www.hotel ribadesellaplaya.com. Right on the beach, this comfortable place has helpful staff and offers particularly good value off season, when it's a **€€**. There's a small supplement for beach views, but it's worth it.
€ Albergue Roberto Frassinelli, C Ricardo Cangas 1, T985 861 105, www.albergue ribadesella.com. Closed Nov. An official YHA hostel in an old beachfront mansion, this characterful place should be booked ahead in summer. They organize all sorts of activities. Reception is only open 1700-2100.

€ **Hotel Covadonga**, C Manuel Caso de la Villa 9, T985 860 110. A good-value and cheerful central place with rooms with or without bath above a convivial bar.

Camping

As well as that listed, there are a couple of campsites with bungalows near the beach. **Ribadesella**, T985 858 293, www.camping-ribadesella.com, in the small village of Sebreño, 1 km inland. Open Apr-Sep. This campsite has more facilities than Los Sauces (the other campsite), including a pool and bungalows.

Llanes p103

The town makes a sound base, with plenty of accommodation and eating choices.
€€ **Hotel Mira-Olas**, Paseo de San Antón 14, T985 400 828, www.hotelmiraolas.com. This quiet hotel is on the eastern side of the harbour and overlooks the colourful cubes. It's been recently refurbished and makes a very pleasant base. The front-facing rooms are large and light.
€€ **Hotel Sablón**, El Sablón s/n, T985 400 787, www.hotelsablon.com. A well-located hotel/restaurant, with views out to sea – perfect for dashing down after breakfast and staking a claim on the tiny beach. The old town is just a few steps away too. Great views from the restaurant terrace.
€€ **La Posada del Rey**, C Mayor 11, T985 401 332, www.laposadadelrey.es. This 6-roomer is a very attractive tiny hotel near the port, decorated with *cariño* and style by an enterprising and energetic old lady. The tiny cute bar is another highlight; off-season rooms are significantly cheaper.
€€ **Pensión La Guía**, C Parres Sobrino 1, T985 402 577, www.pensionlaguia.com. A very pleasant central *pensión* in an old stone building in the heart of town. The rooms are decorated with a sure touch and have modern bathrooms and reading lamps; some have a glassed gallery. There's some noise from the road, but it's worth putting up with. Recommended.

Camping

Camping Entreplayas, Av Toró s/n, T985 400 888. Open Easter-Sep. There are many campsites in the Llanes area. This has a great location on a headland between, as the name gives away, 2 beaches. There are bungalows as well as tent and van sites.

⊘ Eating

Villaviciosa and around p102

Good eating options can be found all along C Generalísimo, rising off the main road behind the town hall. In Tazones, just about anywhere down by the harbour offers good seafood and rice dishes, but beware of the prices, especially in places without a printed menu.
€€ **El Catalín**, La Atalaya 9, Tazones, T985 897 113. On a hill about a kilometre before you reach Tazones from Villaviciosa, this child-friendly place has brilliant views over the village and the wide sea. The seafood rice here is superb and the prices are fair. Recommended.
€€ **El Centollu**, C San Roque 18, Tazones, T985 897 014. There's no menu at this little place, so don't be afraid to ask for prices. The reason there's no menu is a good one though: what's there is whatever was fresh and good that day. Try and bag one of the few outdoor tables. The home-made desserts are really excellent.
€€ **El Congreso de Benjamín**, C Generalísimo 25, T985 892 580. A characteristic Villaviciosa smell of cider permeates this convivial place, which matches considerate service with some excellent seafood eating. Their *navajas* (razor shells) or daily specials are always worth considering; for a blowout, try their *calderetas*; a giant pan for 2 or more that is plonked down awash with fish, prawns, lobster, and garlic aromas.
€€ **El Tonel**, C Alvarez Miranda 13, T985 892 359. On a sidestreet by the park, just up the hill from the big cider house called El Roxu, this is a locals' favourite that offers

Cider House Rules

In contrast to the rest of the nation, where wine and, these days, beer, rules the roost, in Asturias it is cider that Bacchus calls for when refreshment seems needed. Drunk all over the province in thousands of *sidrerías*, *sidra* has developed a complex ritual of its own that at times seems as mysterious as the Japanese tea ceremony. Ordered by the bottle and not by the glass, Asturian cider is a mouth-cleansingly sour tipple containing around 6% alcohol.

The most obvious aspect to the ritual is the method of pouring (the verb is *escanciar*, or decant). It is a case of once seen, never forgotten as the waiter holds aloft the green bottle of cider and pours it from arm's length into a glass without looking. This is done not just for show but to create bubbles in the cider, which are an essential part of the drinking process. The smaller the bubbles the higher the quality of the cider.

The drinker then has a small period of grace known as the *espalmar* during which the bubbles remain in the glass and the small quantity of poured cider must be drunk. This is normally a maximum of 10 seconds. So a leisurely sip is not the norm for Asturian drinkers who usually down the glass or *culín* in one. Normal practice is then to wait until you're ready for another draught, and then give the nod to the eagle-eyed master of ceremonies to refill the glass. However, those feeling a little impatient or emboldened after a bottle or two are welcome to try themselves (at least, that is, in places with a bit of sawdust on the floor, or a trough for spillages). Just be ready to smell of fermented apples for the rest of the evening.

The different types of cider are a result of the various blends of apples used. There are around 20 varieties used in Asturias, each one falling into a different category of sweetness. Usually the cider will be made of 80% dry and semi-dry varieties. The apples are harvested between mid-September and mid-October and important local festivals are based around the harvest. The best known is in Villaviciosa. Another notable cider festival is held in Nava, another cider capital, on 11-12 July.

Not surprisingly, given its importance in Asturian culture, cider is widely used in the local cooking. Most *sidrerías* will produce their own dishes with cider added as a flavouring.

---

excellent value for extremely generous and tasty *raciones* of seafood. The *chipirones* (small cuttlefish) are especially good here, as are the stuffed asparagus.

Lastres and around *p103*

The **Hotel Eutimio** (see Where to stay, page 104) also has a good restaurant.
€€ El Varadero, C Bajada al Puerto s/n, T985 334 032. On the way down to the harbour, this down-to-earth place offers a huge variety of excellent seafood rices, as well as top *chipirones* and other feasts.

Ribadesella *p103*

Head to the old town for characterful eating. Strung around the waterside opposite the *lonja* is a string of places offering seafood and cider at various budget levels.
€€ Arbidel, C Oscura 1, T985 861 440, www.arbidel.com. Tucked away off the main street through town, this lovely little place has the nicest terrace in town and serves a range of rices, fish and meats that offer significant value for this sometimes overpriced summering spot.

€€ El Campanu, C Marqueses de Argüelles 9, T670 603 694. With a cheery terrace, walls painted pastel colours in the *comedor*, and no-nonsense service, this is a reliable choice for seafood in the heart of town. The *campanu* is the first salmon caught in the rivers of Asturias each season.

€€ Sidrería Carroceu, C del Marqués de Argüelles 25, T985 861 419. A good harbourside venue for classy seafood and cider; that typical Asturian combination.

€ Aramburu, Gran Vía s/n, T985 857 626. This great Asturian produce shop is worth a visit for the sights and smells of its tasty range. It's good for a classy picnic, but they also do a range of daily specials in the upstairs dining room.

Llanes *p103*

Most of the action is on C Mayor, where there are many *sidrerías* and restaurants; wander along and take your pick.

€€ El Campanu, La Calzada s/n, T985 401 021. Set on the riverside a block back from the port, this is a good seafood destination. There's an earthy downstairs cider bar, but above is a warmly lit restaurant serving excellent fresh fish. They do a good seafood paella too.

€€ Mesón El Galeón, C Mayor 20. A very good seafood restaurant in the old town near the port. What's on offer depends on the catch. Try the *oricios* (sea urchins) or the grilled meats. There's a gregarious bar downstairs.

€€ Siete Puertas, C Manuel Cue 7, T985 402 751. It's hard to believe that this compact place lives up to its name (7 doors) but it does. But that's not the point; it offers truly delicious meals, with warm seafood salad, for example, making an ideal starter before rice (paella is €44 for 2), fish, seafood, and meat dishes served with solicitous goodwill.

€ Bar Casa del Mar, C del Muelle s/n. Underneath the functional concrete fishermen's club, this place is where locals eat their seafood fresh, simple, and cheap. There's no price gouging; a *ración*

of *langostinos* (king prawns) goes for a bargain €11, *chipirones* are just €5.50, and a memorable *mariscada* for 2, including a bottle of *albariño* wine, costs €75.

⚙ What to do

There are many tour operators on this stretch of coast, typically offering canoeing on the Río Sella, watersports along the beaches, and quad biking or horse riding in the foothills of the Picos de Europa. See also the Picos de Europa section, page 49, for operators offering the canoe descent of the Sella river from Arriondas to Ribadesella.

Ribadesella *p103*

Cuadra El Alisal, T608 104 768. These guys near Ribadesella can organize horse riding from €20 for 1 hr.

Turaventura, Manuel Caso de la Villa 60, T985 560 267, www.turaventura.com. Canoing the Río Sella, and canyoning and caving.

Llanes *p103*
Golf

There's a well-placed seaside links-style golf course east of town, T985 417 230.

Tour operators

Aventura Viesca, T985 357 369, www.aven turaviesca.com. These guys can sort out canyoning, mountaineering, quad biking, and canoeing excursions in the Llanes area.

Escuela Asturiana de Surf, T670 686 801, www.escuelaasturianadesurf.com. Can arrange surfing lessons at a variety of locations on the Asturian coast.

Jaire Aquasport, C El Puerto s/n, T985 841 464. Canoe descents on the Río Sella, as well as mountain biking, caving and guided hiking.

Towards Cantabria *p104*

Devatur, Edificio Estación s/n, Unquera, T942 717 033, www.devatur.com. All kinds of canoeing, rafting and horse-riding activities.

⊖ Transport

Villaviciosa and around *p102*
Bus Several buses a day head to **Oviedo**
and **Gijón**, and some heading east to Lastres.

Lastres and around *p103*
Bus ALSA buses from **Oviedo** and **Gijón**
come several times a day and stop outside
the summer-only tourist office.

Ribadesella *p103*
Bus Ribadesella and Llanes are linked
by bus to **Gijón** and **Oviedo**, and east
to **Santander**.

Llanes *p103*
For buses, see Ribadesella, above. The FEVE
station is to the east of town and is another
means of reaching **Oviedo**, **Gijón** and other
coastal destinations.

Contents

Footnotes

Index

Titles available in the Footprint *Focus* range

Latin America	UK RRP	US RRP
Bahia & Salvador	£7.99	$11.95
Buenos Aires & Pampas	£7.99	$11.95
Costa Rica	£8.99	$12.95
Cuzco, La Paz & Lake Titicaca	£8.99	$12.95
El Salvador	£5.99	$8.95
Guadalajara & Pacific Coast	£6.99	$9.95
Guatemala	£8.99	$12.95
Guyana, Guyane & Suriname	£5.99	$8.95
Havana	£6.99	$9.95
Honduras	£7.99	$11.95
Nicaragua	£7.99	$11.95
Paraguay	£5.99	$8.95
Quito & Galápagos Islands	£7.99	$11.95
Recife & Northeast Brazil	£7.99	$11.95
Rio de Janeiro	£8.99	$12.95
São Paulo	£5.99	$8.95
Uruguay	£6.99	$9.95
Venezuela	£8.99	$12.95
Yucatán Peninsula	£6.99	$9.95

Asia	UK RRP	US RRP
Angkor Wat	£5.99	$8.95
Bali & Lombok	£8.99	$12.95
Chennai & Tamil Nadu	£8.99	$12.95
Chiang Mai & Northern Thailand	£7.99	$11.95
Goa	£6.99	$9.95
Hanoi & Northern Vietnam	£8.99	$12.95
Ho Chi Minh City & Mekong Delta	£7.99	$11.95
Java	£7.99	$11.95
Kerala	£7.99	$11.95
Kolkata & West Bengal	£5.99	$8.95
Mumbai & Gujarat	£8.99	$12.95

Africa & Middle East	UK RRP	US RRP
Beirut	£6.99	$9.95
Damascus	£5.99	$8.95
Durban & KwaZulu Natal	£8.99	$12.95
Fès & Northern Morocco	£8.99	$12.95
Jerusalem	£8.99	$12.95
Johannesburg & Kruger National Park	£7.99	$11.95
Kenya's beaches	£8.99	$12.95
Kilimanjaro & Northern Tanzania	£8.99	$12.95
Zanzibar & Pemba	£7.99	$11.95

Europe	UK RRP	US RRP
Bilbao & Basque Region	£6.99	$9.95
Granada & Sierra Nevada	£6.99	$9.95
Málaga	£5.99	$8.95
Orkney & Shetland Islands	£5.99	$8.95
Skye & Outer Hebrides	£6.99	$9.95

North America	UK RRP	US RRP
Vancouver & Rockies	£8.99	$12.95

Australasia	UK RRP	US RRP
Brisbane & Queensland	£8.99	$12.95
Perth	£7.99	$11.95

For the latest books, e-books and smart phone app releases, and a wealth of travel information, visit us at: www.footprinttravelguides.com.

footprinttravelguides.com

Join us on facebook for the latest travel news, product releases, offers and amazing competitions: www.facebook. com/footprintbooks.com.